Secretly Seeking Sasquatch

A Road Guide to Washington's Bigfoot Country

Jason M. Burke

Copyright ©2019 by Jason M. Burke

All rights reserved, including the right to reproduce this book or portions thereof in any form whatsoever.

ISBN: 9781086659115
Independently Published
Cover design by Seyi Paul, teamjunho on fiverr.com

You may contact the author at
secretlyseekingsasquatch@gmail.com

Dedication

To Grandma, who taught me to fish and inspired me to hunt monsters. You are dearly missed.

Contents

Dedication

Acknowledgments

Chance Encounters

Bumps in the Night

My Monster Pedigree

Olympic Peninsula

It was the Summer of '69!

The Northern Cascades

Southwest Washington

Over the River and Through the Wood

The Skookums of Skamania County

An Ape by any other Name

Thar Be Mountain Devils Here!

Mount Saint Helens Part 2 This Time it's Personal

Wired for Weird

The Ballad of Criplefoot

The Land of Okanogan

Impression Pun

    Camera:

    Recording Sound:

    Recording Physical Evidence:

    Casting Prints:

    Must-Have:

Nice to Have:

Money is no option…you have a rich benefactor funding your research efforts:

Pareidolia the Destroyer

Bigfoot: How I see Him/Her/It/Them

Advice to a Noob from an Intermediate Noob

Sasquatch Sins

Wally, the Wildman of Walla Walla Washington

The Rabbit Hole

The Search for Us

The Maps

The Olympic Peninsula

    Lake Quinault M1

    The Hoh Rainforest M2

    Dosewallips Road M3

    Dekay Road M4

    Lake Cushman M5

Northern Cascades

    Mount Baker M6

    Barlow Pass M7

Southwest Washington

    Capitol Forest M8

    Chehalis to Raymond M9

Land of the Skookum

    Thar be Mountain Devils Here M10

    Curly Creek Road M11

    Wind River Road M12

    Skamania County M13

Over the River and Through the Wood (South)

    Chinook Pass M14

Throwing you for a Loop M15

Over the River and Through the Wood (North)

    Stevens Pass M16

Land of the Okanogan

    Chopaka Lake M17

    Sherman Pass M18

    Disautel Pass M19

Walla Walla

    Five Points M20

    Kendall Skyline Road (KSR) M21

Acknowledgments

None of this would have been possible without the love, support and confidence showed to me by my wife and kids. I love you guys more than Bigfoot!

Chance Encounters

You're cruising down a wooded road. You are enjoying your drive and are caught up in the beauty Washington State has to offer. You near the crest of a hill and round a blind corner. Your eyes dart instantly to something along the guardrail. It can't be a tree stump, it's in the road. A rock? It's an animal. Dog? Deer? Elk? Bear? Every possibility darts through your mind in mere fractions of a second. Your foot finds the brake pedal and the car stops suddenly. It's standing up! Is it a man in a fur coat? My god, it's huge! A gorilla? It just looked at me. Then the large, hair-covered "something" walks briskly into the forest on two legs.

Figure 1: Caught in the Headlights. Illustration (watercolor) by author.

Among the hundreds of recorded sightings in the Pacific Northwest, this type of encounter is not uncommon. Whether the witness was a skeptic or believer prior to the event they are left shaken and dumbfounded. Their brain struggles to make sense of what their eyes have just seen.

I have reviewed every account of Bigfoot I could find. I've read the books, studied websites, attended presentations, and whenever possible, I have interviewed witnesses and the top researchers. I've even stayed nights in the field with world-renowned scientists and Yeti trackers! I want to put you into the heart of Sasquatch country.

Sightings, by and large, take place in or near heavily forested areas and, most often, not far from a freshwater source. For every report where I could determine a specific location, I marked it on a map. It wasn't long before patterns emerged and it was clear to me that one could navigate Bigfoot's domain via Washington's paved roads and highways.

During my research, I was met with a dilemma. Which reports do I use and which do I throw out? I tried to remain as objective as possible but there were some reports, for one reason or another, I simply did not believe. Those were the reports that made my "Ranger Sense" tingle. Something didn't smell right.

It's also important to note that not all reports are sightings. Much of what I reviewed equated to a personal experience. Something had affected the witness in such a way that they attributed it to Bigfoot and felt compelled to file a report. Personal experiences seem to range from sounds to smells to an uneasy feeling of being watched. I scrutinized these harshly but they always seemed to fall into geographical regions that were corroborated with sightings and footprint finds (or other physical evidence). While I suspect a high number of personal encounters can be attributed to more common sources than Sasquatch (coyote, elk, bear, and barred owl for example), a substantial amount of intriguing experiences are derived from witnesses who shouldn't be easily fooled. A perfect example would be the long-time local with outdoors experience that has a comprehensive understanding of the local fauna and the sounds forest animals make and the behavior they exhibit. Anything atypical would stick out and this witness would be qualified to report the anomaly credibly.

Most of the reports I read had already been scrutinized by some sort of filter. Reputable researchers and authors explained which reports were less than believable and which sources weren't all that credible. So, I rejected those. In addition to many published works, I utilized the website: Bigfoot Research Organization (BFRO.net). One cannot post anonymously on the BFRO rather, their reports are submitted for review to a researcher who evaluates the case, personally interviews each witness and then decides if it is credible enough to post on the site. The witness can then choose to remain anonymous.

Consider this: how many Bigfoot experiences go *unreported*? Any witness is faced with a gambit of questions and concerns. Who should I tell? Who would believe me? Folks will think I'm crazy. I don't want to be one of THOSE people.

Lastly, I've come to understand that some communities are more tight-lipped than others. I believe small logging towns and reservations are perfect examples of this tendency. They (collectively) are content with keeping these stories within their own community. This is certainly not a sin. I just think it merits mentioning that books, articles, and databases are but the tip of a hairy iceberg.

I was unprepared for how believable most of these accounts were. They consisted of average people performing normal acts and encountering something extraordinary. I'm taking you to these areas. In some cases, you'll be in the exact place where the event occurred. You'll visit towns steeped in local whimsical Bigfoot culture. You'll find Sasquatch photo ops. Unless otherwise noted, these routes should be within the abilities of an average family sedan. I personally explored them in a Ford Focus. Be conscious of seasonal closures and weather conditions and please, drive carefully. Do not trespass and be respectful. Load your kids in the car and have some fun.

Simply put, your best chance of seeing Bigfoot is to visit Bigfoot country and I know Bigfoot country.

There aren't a great number of true scientists in the field conducting Bigfoot

Figure 2: A warning sign near Chopaka.

research. I can find no evidence that there are any government or university-funded studies into the search for Sasquatch currently underway. There are amateurs, researchers with impressive pedigrees, a few Ph.D.'s spending their own dime, and a group of people coined *citizen scientists*. Also, there are a few kooks out there committing heinous hoaxes and/or practicing junk science which damages credibility to the field in general. For all those warm bodies, the true sightings seem to come by accident. Many are by the motorist. This is why I've enlisted you. YOU have as good of a chance of witnessing a Sasquatch as the woodsman who takes pack mules into the Goat Rocks Wilderness or the habituators[1] who camp every weekend in the Gifford Pinchot. By driving these routes, incorporating them into your vacations or just doing a little exploring, I honestly believe you have a chance to catch a glimpse of the extremely rare creature.

I guarantee that someone who uses this book will have an experience that they can chalk up to Bigfoot. Let's start the search.

---

[1] Researchers who frequent one area, often camping, and try to lure Sasquatch to them. This practice rests on the idea of gaining trust and the creature in-question actually getting to recognize the regular visitors.

Jason M. Burke

Bumps in the Night

Do you believe in UFOs, astral projections, mental telepathy, ESP, clairvoyance, spirit photography, telekinetic movement, full trance mediums, the Loch Ness monster and the theory of Atlantis?

-Janine Melnitz (Annie Potts), Ghostbusters

I lie in bed groggily listening to the drunken upstairs neighbor stumble home with more than one anonymous drinking companion. I remember the precise time: 2:42 a.m. As his door slammed inconsiderately shut I heard a "rustling". What happened next? I cannot fully explain. I can only report the facts to you. The closet lit up with a soft green light. Some source of illumination (I hesitate to call it an orb but everything about it was spherical in nature) traveled from the closet's ceiling through, THROUGH the floor beneath. It did not fall, it traveled slowly but deliberately. My wife rolled over and said to me "did you hear that sound?" To which my reply was "did you see the weird green light in the closet?!" Unfortunately, she had not. She had, however, heard the noise, which I attribute to the strange light somehow disrupting items in its path through the closet. The sphere, you see, seemed to have some physicality. I spent the next hour digging through the closet. I was searching for a logical explanation to what I'd just seen. I was half expecting to find a puddle of ectoplasm like Slimer left in *Ghostbusters*[2]. It was as though some unseen intruder had hidden out of sight and hoaxed me with a glow-stick. I won't go through any great detail trying to argue against the terrestrial explanations that are going through your head right now. It was not some wholly explainable or logical light source. In a large brick and concrete building at the center of a closed 316-acre park, I can tell you it wasn't a reflection or passing headlights nor was it a hallucination (at least I'm not prone to hallucinations --that I know of--) and I swear I am not lying. You'll never be able to convince me that I didn't *see* what I *saw* or that I simply misidentified something else. I researched a sleep disorder termed *hypnogogic* wherein the subject experiences dream imagery within a transitional state of consciousness. Meaning: it takes a moment to shake off the dream images just after you're technically awake. If there weren't any other corroborative evidence, I'd accept this but as you'll read much later, this wasn't the green orb's only appearance. The only word that vaguely describes the phenomenon I witnessed is *ghost*. I know it wasn't swamp gas and I doubt it was ball lightning. What I saw was EXTRAORDINARY and defied any reasonable explanation I could assign. I witnessed something that, by all accounts, shouldn't be.

What does this have to do with Bigfoot? Absolutely nothing.

I kid of course. But my point is: there are unexplained and undiscovered wonders left in the world. Someday they will have an explanation, a scientific name and a commonplace alongside humanity. What was once *paranormal* will join the normal. But for now, they remain out there on the fringe, at the edge of what our brains can comprehend as tangible and always retreating back to the Goblin Universe.[3]

Please don't construe that I consider the elusive hominid (or hominoid)[4] to be paranormal. But given the centuries of folklore and mystery without a

---

[2] While we're on the subject of Ghostbusters, did anyone else notice that in the animated version, *The Real Ghostbusters*, the actor who supplied Dr. Peter Venkman's voice (Bill Murray from the movie) was the same guy who supplied the voice of Garfield in *Garfield and Friends* (Lorenzo Music)? Conversely, Bill Murray then voiced Garfield in the "live action" movie. I can't be the only one who noticed that!

[3] Describing a realm of mythical creatures and paranormal enigmas, *the Goblin Universe* is a term that has been used by monster hunters and authors since the mid-1960's to try to group the strange oddities that seem to go along with a mystery like the Loch Ness Monster or Sasquatch.

[4] Hominid: closer to human than any ape. Hominoid: a great ape, i.e. gorilla, chimpanzee or orangutan.

definitive specimen, it's hardly inexcusable to think of this creature in the Fortean[5] context.

Sasquatch has undergone a significant image change in the 21st Century. When Bigfoot mania hit its fever pitch in the 1950s and '60s, the media billed it as a monster. This stigma would follow Bigfoot for decades. In fact, "Big Foot" was a mere nickname coined by locals in Humboldt County, California for whoever was stomping around and leaving the giant, human-like footprints. The moniker was sensationalized and shortened to one word by columnist Andrew Ginzoli when the *Humboldt Times* ran a story about a rash of mysterious footprints turning up as a road construction crew cut into previously unlogged woods. It was an era devoid of the internet and the level of unavoidable information-contagion we have today. This was the first time many Americans had even heard of the elusive mountain ape even though accounts predate colonization. So, in October 1958, a monster was born.

Believers and non-believers are still divergently polarized but I think the issue is mostly debated along the lines of "Bigfoot is an animal which may, or may not exist.[6]" Scientific discoveries of some pretty substantial animals have given the faithful something for which to cling. The coelacanth, gorilla, and saola (a large Vietnamese deer) were all known by locals but not accepted by science until the 20th century.

Perhaps the most encouraging, not to mention the most recent, lesson comes in the form of the Bili ape. Congolese locals had spun yarns about the "lion killers," an aggressive ape species that science just hadn't gotten around to yet. In fact, at the time Dr. Jeff Meldrum[7] was writing *Sasquatch: Legend Meets Science*, the Bili ape was but a cryptid "with little more evidence to go on than some oversized footprints, nests, a few strands of hair, and persistent native accounts." Sound familiar? (Meldrum, p. 592 digital edition)

Swiss photographer, and anti-bushmeat activist, Karl Ammann, in search of Gorillas, found a skull that seemed to have some chimp-like features but was different in many regards. He then examined a poacher's trail camera footage of what looked like giant chimpanzees. The Congo, being as unstable politically as it is dauntingly inaccessible, obstructed scientific efforts for half a decade.

---

[5] Charles Fort was an American writer who delved into anomalous phenomena, so much so that the term *Fortean* is often attributed to phenomena of this nature.

[6] After becoming more attuned to Bigfoot culture, I found this to be partially untrue. I discuss this later but Bigfoot believers are largely polarized between "flesh and blood" and a *being* of paranormal properties.

[7] Professor of Anatomy and Anthropology and a Professor of the Department of Anthropology at **Idaho State University**.

Secretly Seeking Sasquatch

Foreigners were faced with *guerilla* problems, not *gorilla*. Meanwhile, ground nest discoveries kept interests kindled (Roach, 2003). Finally, members of a scientific research team representing the Wildlife Conservation Society and Harvard University mounted an expedition. Deep into the jungle the team heard the chimp noises before they actually saw the elusive apes. The apes appeared swiftly in a very aggressive charge. Much to the humans' mutual relief, it was a bluff charge and the apes retreated.

The ground nests and strange fecal samples observed and recorded ring very true for the Sasquatch enigma. What came of this ape discovery was the Bili ape, a larger chimp cousin. Please do an internet search along the lines of "first Bili ape video" You'll find trail cam footage and video of one in a tree. For those who claim video evidence will never "prove" Bigfoot. Well, video of this quality would go a long way. That skull is the seemingly unobtainable glass slipper. We need that Sasquatch bone, be it a molar or even part of a pinky would do! The lesson to take home though is the presence of the following: cultural stories, strange fecal remains, eyewitness testimony, noises unlike the other forest animals, and ground nests. Let's not forget footprints!

***

Could an ancient apelike-manlike cousin have escaped both extinction and mainstream discovery since the time that humans started acting "human?" The smart money says "no." But I can say with great conviction and authority that there is definitely *something* to undiscovered phenomena. I'm not saying I buy into fairies or leprechauns, flying squirrels or even the Loch Ness Monster but I do earnestly believe there are a few cryptids among us and Bigfoot is the Holy Grail of them all.

My reaction to the event that occurred that dark, early morning was not unique. It turned my world upside down. It indelibly altered my perception of the world. Previously, I'd been on the fence about ghosts. I approach most of these subjects with an air of agnosticism. I was open to the possibility of a haunting phenomenon, but I wasn't (and am still not) very quick to say that ghosts are the spirits of the once-living. But here it was, a green glowing *something* had floated precariously downward in my closet disturbing the closet's contents and my sense of reality all at once.

People who witness Bigfoot report the same life-altering paradigm shift. Most often they didn't *want to* or *plan on* experiencing what they experienced. It had simply happened to them and there was but one explanation: we share this land with large, hairy neighbors and they each walk on two legs.

I realize I'm on dancing in a minefield here discussing ghosts and Bigfoot in the same chapter. What I saw was *there*. *Ghost* is a word. I cannot prove nor test that the thing I saw or the phenomenon I witnessed was the soul of the dead any more than I can prove that humans, or all living things for that matter, even have souls.

Cryptozoology deals with unknown and undiscovered <u>animals</u>. Chad Arment is careful to draw the distinction: "cryptids are often sandwiched between ghosts and UFO's within documentary-style programming creating the perception that they are unearthly or paranormal." He goes on "Paranormal folkloric entities, whether ghosts, vampires, or lycanthropes, are not cryptozoological" (Arment, p. 11). He's right. The "zoology" part is a dead giveaway. I was very careful, though, how I described my sighting of what could be called a ghost. I don't presume to know *what* exactly was in front of me. It didn't exhibit any of the biological traits attributed to animals. All I can tell you is: it was there.

So paranormal investigation may have an even more taboo reputation than cryptozoology but since you're quite literally going to read about UFO's (technically an *unidentified flying object* wouldn't be as taboo as *an extra-terrestrial vehicle*) and the green mystery orb, albeit briefly, in the following chapters, understand that I'm driving home the point: something happened that defied contemporary scientific explanation. The only graspable definition is the one that only some, not all, will believe.

What if some of these witnesses are telling the truth? How would you react if your most trusted confidant told you such a story?

A note on nomenclature: I'm going to use the terms *Bigfoot* and *Sasquatch* interchangeably. I firmly believe that someday this creature will be a recognized catalog entry among the world's beasties and that the terms "Bigfoot" or "Sasquatch" may seem old-fashioned, inappropriate or even derogatory. You'll also see "wood ape," "mountain ape," and just plain old "ape." That's not to say that I don't believe that the creature: Sasquatch might be a lost tribe of people not too far separated from *Homo sapiens*. I'm using "ape" in the broadest sense. I'm a great ape, a descendant from ancestral apes. Furthermore, *Bigfoot* can be both singular and plural. I favor Loren Coleman's treatment of pluralizing Bigfoot (Coleman, Cryptomundo.com, 2006). The word *Bigfoots* drives me crazy.

Also, we're going to move forward on some pre-agreed-upon assumptions:

1. There exists a population of Sasquatch capable of healthfully reproducing via good old-fashioned male-female interaction.

2. My treatment of the creature: Sasquatch, is one of a terrestrial being of flesh and blood.

These caveats will limit my "if/then" statements, which I'm famous for in conversation but the habit would be maddening in print. So, there shouldn't be too may sentences constructed with: <u>If</u> Sasquatch exists <u>then</u>. Furthermore, I'm not going to spend a great deal of time trying to prove Bigfoot's existence or persuading you to believe. This is not that type of book and the subject has been debated ad nauseam. I would hesitate to say there are a lot of books available on the Bigfoot mystery but I will say that the vast majority of those address the same questions concerning Sasquatch's existence, anecdotal behavior, possible origin and *why the heck hasn't anyone found any bones?* It would be redundant of me to address those issues and I am neither a biologist nor anthropologist. Please consult the bibliography for further readings.

There may be a contingent that will nitpick at my arguments and suggest, that, for example, if I throw out the paranormal and supernatural accounts of Bigfoot encounters, I'm only making Bigfoot more believable to support my belief in their existence. It is my belief that the creature known as Sasquatch is a creature of flesh and blood and is limited by the same set of natural laws and physics that we are. There are people who believe Bigfoot may be an extraterrestrial or inter-dimensional visitor or skinwalker. This is all well and good except for the fact that I don't know how to look for one of those creatures. Do you? I'm not sure I even know how to look for a North American ape but, so long as I feel it needs water to drink, food to eat, and can't summon a wormhole via telepathic command, then I feel I have at least a statistical chance of seeing one. Imbuing this creature with teleportational abilities only clutters my mind with questions to which I don't have the answers. Why would this creature only quantum leap into the deep dark woods and foothills? Wouldn't one occasionally misjudge the mind-bogglingly difficult mathematics and suddenly appear at your daughter's dance recital or in front of a curbside pretzel truck?!

Secretly Seeking Sasquatch

You've read this disclaimer and know I'm going to intentionally and willfully lay it all out there. You don't have to believe in Bigfoot to enjoy this book. I respect your opinion. This book is meant to give you and your family a truly unique (hopefully) and fun (mostly) way of approaching Washington's wonders and driving her scenic byways.

Jason M. Burke

My Monster Pedigree

I was born in 1973 at the tail end of an era that was truly a Bigfoot enthusiast's heyday and growing up, I watched all of the old documentaries on the paranormal and the unknown. To me, the cream of the crop was *In Search Of*. Do you remember this show? It was hosted by Leonard Nimoy and delved into matters of the eerie and unexplained. It was freakin' Spock telling me about The Loch Ness Monster! The Bigfoot episodes of *In Search Of* are gems and should be required viewing for any enthusiast. They are waiting for you on YouTube.

Much of my childhood was centered on and around the only lake in Whitman County, Washington. About 17 million years ago a volcano in southern Idaho (not then *Idaho*) barfed up enough basaltic lava to cover much of the inland areas of the Pacific Northwest. At the end of the last ice age (about 15,000 years ago) an ice dam holding an enormous glacial lake burst in what is now Missoula, Montana. Depending on which anthropologist or archeologist you speak to, this was about the time our human ancestors were migrating across the Bering land bridge. It is also hypothesized by some that another ape migrated here at the same time.

In a natural disaster that was catastrophic beyond all human reckoning, the torrent of floodwaters rapidly carved through the basalt and left the scablands of Washington with frequent oases by way of lakes, canyons, and waterfalls of which Rock Lake is one. My ancestors homesteaded the area, not far from St John, Washington (some years later of course) and the lake and its surrounding hills and valleys provided rich farming, hunting, and fishing grounds as well as recreational respite. The lake is deep, dark and treacherous. It fills the depth of a basalt canyon, a deep one, but there are submerged bluffs. Many-a-boater has sheered their props or run aground as their depth-finders jumped from hundreds of feet in depth to hip-deep water in mere seconds. The water is cold and being in a very remote area, your hope of rescue is nil. The lake has its share of deaths by drowning and, if I may sound like an old enigmatic sea captain for a moment, *one eye squinted* "she does not give up her dead." This is where the monster comes in.

Visit nearly any American small town, settlement, reservation or battlefield and there's sure to be a few paranormal tales within their local mythos. Haven't you heard stories of a magic hill where cars roll "up," a phantom hitchhiker, a forlorn spirit, a prophetic Mothman, or a demonic winged devil? Tales of lake monsters don't seem any less common though few have the notoriety of Nessie in Scotland or Ogopogo in Okanagan Lake, B.C.

Rock Lake's resident serpent, aptly named "The Rock Lake Monster," has been blamed for any number of drowning and locals have even had their share of sightings. Among them, my great grandfather (my mother's maternal grandfather), Fred Wagner spoke of seeing a creature thrashing about the surface with a reptilian back like an alligator[8]. Common among most monster tales, sources quote my great grandfather as being a "religious man, not prone to lying." My grandfather (my mother's father, Pete) told his own tale. While bird hunting the bluffs above the lake, he shot a ringneck rooster (pheasant) that unfortunately nose-dived some sixty feet into the water below. Pete peered over the bluff to see if the game bird was retrievable and was astonished to see the floating bird pulled under multiple times. Something was manipulating the bird and, as he would tell the story "pheasants don't dive." He was convinced an animal had interfered with the dead bird in search of a meal and fish in Rock Lake just shouldn't get that large (but they do get large). So, some decades later in my grade school years, my grandparents and my mom would entertain me with these tales. The murky waters of that lake simultaneously scared and captivated me and I looked for the monster a lot. My grandfather was an extremely intelligent man and had a solid reputation as a farmer, inventor, and visionary. He wasn't quick to blame a monster or anything else supernatural for the strange occurrences. His theory was that the culprit was a sturgeon. Whether introduced or extremely lost, this prehistoric sea-going leviathan would seem to match the saurian physical description and while not a predatory fish, could have the requisite size and mystique to frighten the local inhabitants. Moreover, Rock Creek which drains out of Rock Lake, squirms around and flows into the Palouse River. The Palouse River slithers through the sagebrush down to the Snake River (see what I did there?) and then the Snake

---

[8] My mother reported to me that both her Grandfather and his hired hand witnessed creatures, plural; three obtusely long shapes swimming beneath the murky green water. The men climbed down to investigate and the creatures were gone.

dumps its water into the Columbia, which is Sturgeonville, USA. It's all Pacific Ocean from there. There are formidable barriers, one being the Palouse Falls but nature routinely finds a workaround.

Figure 3: My grandad, Pete, as a boy standing atop the bluffs at Rock Lake. Photographer unknown.

Somewhere in my childish mind, I had equated the Rock Lake Monster to the photo (then believable) of Nessie as her head neck and body are seen silhouetted against the ripples of a calm day on the loch[9]. The photo suggests the creature is a plesiosaur. I would draw countless pictures of a serpent's head and neck slinking up from the water's surface and proclaim to everyone "this is a sturgeon…this is the Rock Lake Monster!"

My grandfather grew sick. There were times he was unable to join us on fishing adventures. Many times, it was just my grandma and me exploring the land and fishing seldom visited holes. We'd fish from the bank at Rock Lake and she'd encourage me to keep a lookout for the monster. Further back, when everyone was healthy, we'd take an aluminum barge, which my grandfather had built from surplus military equipment and troll the many deep-water chasms for the elusive rainbow trout lunkers below. There again, every log, every ripple or boat wake fell within the focus of my binoculars for hopes of glimpsing a monster.

It's important to describe my grandma, Marge, as she was so influential in the development of my mystery curiosity. She didn't knit. She didn't collect doilies. She was artistic and painted farmland oil paintings and took ceramics classes where she produced glazed Christmas decorations, animal figurines and many novelty whiskey flasks. She almost always had a fat German Shepard named "Queen," at least three (one at a time over the many years) that I can remember. Any second dog was named "Cricket." This was a strict rule she stubbornly adhered to only having broken it on two occasions: a dumped stray dachshund she named Marvin and a fat German Shepard that, after my mom filed an injunction in court, was able to convince Grandma to name the dog Sally.

She was the last of a generation of frontiersmen (frontierswomen) long before ranch life became modernized, before cell phones and the internet. I can remember when the ranch house got a telephone. She lived on that ranch, alone, for years after my grandfather died. She had, at the ready, a break-action, single-shot .410 shotgun. Taped to the barrel was the first rechargeable spotlight Black and Decker ever produced. In addition to protecting herself, she could very confidently use this gun to protect her chickens from troublesome owls or

---

[9] Known as "the Surgeon's Photo" he (the surgeon/witness) confessed to have hoaxed the photo with a modified toy submarine although the truthfulness of the confession is also up for debate. (Jeans, 1995)

raccoons. She drank bourbon and water, most often the two combined. I'm telling you she was tough[10].

Figure 4: Grandad and Grandma trolling from the barge.
Photographer: Linda Burke

Why have I shared this story with you? It has nothing to do with Bigfoot. I just wanted you to understand that cryptozoology was kind of in my blood. While I was researching this book in what was one of the hundreds of strange coincidences, I happened upon a chapter about the Rock Lake Monster. I was a little stunned to find everything I'd been told as a kid appear in print. In fact, my relatives had been mentioned. Undoubtedly the author had read an old newspaper article from which my family had been interviewed and photographed at the public landing at the lake[11]. While very young, my sister and I were in

---

[10] I'm not saying the consumption of alcohol makes one tough, rather, I'm saying it was a character trait which her contemporaries would associate with "toughness" at the time.

[11] The story appeared in Strange Monsters of the Pacific Northwest by Michael Newton (pp. 66-67). It references an article in the *Whitman County Gazette* (then *Colfax Gazette*).The book, for reasons not known to me, refers to my Grandfather as "Leroy" but his name was actually Floyd and everyone called him "Pete." The story may not appear in later editions of this book.

attendance that day and marveled at the tales told about haunted waters. The Big Swede, a railroad man, who had famously disappeared while attempting to swim the lake's width on a bet and the steam locomotive carrying brand new Model T Fords that catastrophically derailed and crashed into the lake, disappeared below the surface and was never recovered and of course, tales of the monster. Also present on that day was another enthusiastic "witness" who claimed the creature came ashore and dragged his poor dog back into the lake like some B horror movie. My family would later refer to this unsolicited witness as a crazy drunk.

This was the late '70s, pre-Mount Saint Helens eruption. Actually, I have an entire story about how I survived the eruption which involves my family having to walk, through a barren ash-covered wasteland from Rock Lake to the tiny town of Ewan to seek refuge from the falling ash but I'll spare you that story. Anyway, my grandfather had arrived at his sturgeon theory independently. It was years later that I would see the sturgeon theory being kicked around on mystery reality shows like *River Monsters* and *Monsterquest*. I'd have to wait until I was a middle-aged man and my grandfather had been gone almost 30 years before I realized how much he'd influenced me. He nurtured in me a critical, yet open mind and a strong will to take on a compelling mystery, the whole time sifting through the most obvious and logical explanations first. From him, I inherited a strong sense of adventure and a penchant for misadventure.

So, through my elementary school years, I was monster-crazy. My mother, intelligent and progressive, encouraged my interest and, like many kids of the day, I checked out every book I could find on Bigfoot and lake monsters from my little elementary school's library. Then from my teens on into adulthood, my interest cooled for a while. My personal cynicism and prejudices kicked in and Sasquatch didn't fare well. There, the beast was very nearly lost.

Flash forward to my paranormal paradigm shift, who was I now to doubt what I couldn't see? Bigfoot crept back into my consciousness. As a Park Ranger, for the first time, I was actually working in classic Bigfoot country. I subconsciously kept a lookout for the creatures in my peripheral vision as I drove the coastal roads or hiked on down the trail. Then, throw into the mix that I got married and had some kids, magic had reentered my life. Kids are full of imagination and wonder and it's so darn easy to rediscover your childhood through their open eyes and untainted hearts. Bigfoot became real to me again. Serendipitously, reality shows like *Monsterquest, Finding Bigfoot* and *Destination Truth* made monster-hunting cool (at least I think so). A spark in me had been rekindled and like that child some three decades ago, I began to read books and pour myself into the subject matter again.

Oddly enough, at about the same time, my sister's interest in the subject reemerged. I don't know how or why. I hadn't shared my interest with her. We each had arrived at it seemingly simultaneously and coincidentally. So, it was on Thanksgiving, 2012, when my sister and her family had trekked across the mountains for the first time to see my family's new home near Seattle. There was a *Finding Bigfoot* marathon on Animal Planet. She turned to me and said, "on the way over here, I was looking at the trees expecting Bigfoot to walk out." Now, in my mind, I was admittedly critical of my sister's statement. I thought to myself: I highly doubt Bigfoot is going to risk a public appearance on a holiday weekend along Interstate 90. But a seed began to grow in my mind. Bigfoot *must* cross roads, right? There are plenty of sightings from automobiles. Has anyone ever written a roadside guide to Bigfoot? No! At least none that I could find (at the time). I read as many Bigfoot books as I could get my hands on. About this, I posted the following Facebook update: "Barnes and Noble have an entire section devoted to *Teen Paranormal Romance* but not a single book on Bigfoot!" Furthermore, most of the books available take a decidedly scientific or paranormal approach organized chronologically or categorically. It is my intent to take on the challenge of organizing Washington's sightings geographically and providing reasonably accessible driving routes which a family could enjoy on a road trip.

So, who is this book for? Well, I mentioned that you don't have to *believe* in Bigfoot to enjoy this guide. That statement comes with a caveat. If you're a skeptic, you can still enjoy this book. If you're a staunch non-believer but you have a child or children, you can still enjoy this book if you're willing to nourish your children's imaginations. However, if you are intent on closing the same doors in your child's mind that are closed in yours, then this book is not for you. I'd still encourage you to read it but I hope you appreciate me giving you a point to bail out here. If you're a Bigfoot true-believer or devoted fan, or even an agnostic then, welcome to the club and please read on. If you're a Bigfoot Researcher, amateur or otherwise, then this book should be in your car. Let's have an adventure.

Olympic Peninsula

The night was moist. This phrase, borrowed from Larry (Billy Crystal) in *Throw Momma from the Train*, very profoundly describes my experiences on the Olympic Peninsula. It rains a lot here. A lot. When I was first cutting my ranger teeth I did a stint near Ocean Shores in Grays Harbor County. I had left the rolling farmland of Eastern Washington. My assessment of the coastal weather was this: It's like being constantly *misted* with a spray bottle. I enjoy this sensation about as much as a housecat. But it does get nice here, very nice. It's this balance of significant rainfall, mild temperatures and a-little-more-than-occasional sunshine that makes this such a favorable climate for an undiscovered mountain ape. There are ample food and habitat.

In an interview with *USA Today* by Larry Blieberg, Bigfoot Researcher, Matt Moneymaker reported that the best Bigfoot area in Washington was the Olympic Peninsula (Bleiberg, 2012). I had an opportunity to interview Moneymaker's contemporary, Cliff Barackman of Animal Planet's *Finding Bigfoot*. I asked him where, in his opinion, was the best place in Washington to drive and hope to see Bigfoot from the car. He said "Logging roads at night on the Olympic Peninsula. The habitat is perfect, and largely unused at night."

So, I found myself, one dark (very dark) and rainy (very rainy) night on one such logging road. Trying my best to track down the site of an eyewitness report my little a car and I left the pavement near Humptulips and I hoped to catch a glimpse of the beast somewhere in the wilds along the river. I was looking, REALLY looking for Sasquatch. It was far too dark to search for physical evidence or photo ops. In the driving rain, my only real hope was to illuminate the creature with my headlights. The road twisted and narrowed. The alders and ferns and salal crept so far into the roadway now that the vegetation brushed my windows as I slowly inched on. Obviously, I had long left behind what could be considered a recently traveled road. Then I got the creeps. You have to know what I mean right? It was only earlier in the day I had found a strange footprint, of which I mention later in this chapter. My nerves were already frayed. I got spooked. In my mind's eye, I pictured Bigfoot's wet, dark hand touching the window nearest me. What would I do? Flee? Certainly. I had no doubt now that, should this animal present itself, I would respond in hasty retreat. With as narrow as the road was, I'd have to execute this maneuver in reverse. Now, I don't like to brag but I was, by a wide margin, the best reverse-driver in my academy's EVOC[12]. But there were too many adverse variables in play for me to place any confidence there. I chickened out. Are you happy? I did not at that moment wish to witness a Sasquatch. I was there alone and, like the ten-year-old-kid that couldn't make it all night camped out in the yard, fled for the comfort of the indoors. I vowed to bring a companion on future night explorations.

***

U.S. 101 loops the Peninsula and is listed in many guidebooks as one of Washington's top scenic drives. It seems a reasonable assumption that all peninsula Sasquatch have to cross this road sooner or later and many reports reflect this. Keep your eyes open around the town of Humptulips and the river by the same name. Neilton and Quinault are also towns known to produce hairy biped reports (BFRO #14112).

Figure 5: Photo op! Gnarly wood carvings outside a motel along WA 109.

---

[12] Emergency Vehicle Operation Course

Making the loop along Lake Quinault (M1) on the North Shore and South Shore roads is an absolute must and provides ample opportunities to view waterfalls, bald eagles, deer, and herds of Roosevelt Elk[13]. If you look beneath the vampire lore surrounding the little town of Forks, you'll probably find a healthy stratum of Sasquatch history (BFRO #6058). The river valleys of The Hoh (M2), Queets, Dungeness, Elwah, and Wynoochee would seem to offer a substantial food source to a Sasquatch during the salmon runs and possibly serve as a thoroughfare through which to travel. Sasquatch has even been reported gathering clams on the beach.

Between 2000 and 2002 sightings and footprints were reported in the areas of the Hoh Indian Reservation and Forks (Coleman, Bigfoot! The True Story of Apes in America, p. 10). This area is known in Bigfoot legend for producing one of the most credible reports to emerge during the 1960s. Cruising home from a

Figure 6: Washington's storm-battered coast. Unless indicated, all photographs are by the author.

call, a Grays Harbor Sheriff's deputy named Verlin Herrington took DeKay Road in route to his residence in Copalis, WA (M4). According to the August 17, 1969 edition of *The Ocean Observer*, it was 2:35 in the morning and as he rounded a corner, a big hairy *something* appeared before him. Herrington, well aware of the appearance of the local fauna, could apply no other explanation to his sighting than Bigfoot. This was no bear. He kept quiet for the most part but confided in two fellow officers where the conversation was overheard in a café. From there the encounter erupted into a media frenzy which resulted in the sheriff's

---

[13] Roosevelt Elk are the largest subspecies of the North American elk and are found in the rain forests near the Olympic Mountains.

department offering an official position that Herrington had seen a bear (Green, The Best of Bigfoot Sasquatch, pp. 66-67). Deputy Herrington, however, never changed his story and even toured the scene with Bigfoot researchers. If you've ever wondered why witnesses are reluctant to tell their tales, Deputy Herrington's contract was not renewed by the sheriff's department the following year. If you follow the trail of breadcrumbs, it would seem his stance on Bigfoot cost him his job (Bord, p. 110).

An excellent question-and-answer interview between researcher John Green and Herrington is printed in Green's: *Sasquatch* (Green, Sasquatch: The Apes Among Us, pp. 402-403).

Secretly Seeking Sasquatch

In the mid-1960s, again in the Copalis area, a logger family ran afoul of a Bigfoot. The father of the family was a well-respected and very intelligent timberman who worked on cedar salvage permits. The cedar was milled into shakes in the city of Aberdeen. The man and his wife had two boys ages twelve and four. The youngest boy was the first to see "The Copalis Cowman" as it would later be known. The boy called it a cowman because it was covered in hair and smelled bad, like the cows.

Figure 7: Photo op! A Sasquatch crossing on Lincoln Street in Hoquiam.

The family had several frightening encounters with the creature (or possibly 2 creatures) over the ensuing days. Several aggressive incidents directed toward the twelve-year-old and the father had them in fear for their lives. Their house was ransacked. Perhaps the most disturbing fact was that a creature, according to the four-year-old, would come to his window at night and "speak" to him. The creature made gentle "ooh's" and "eehs's." He said it could whistle like a bird and snort just like the pigs. The mother actually witnessed the creature at her son's window and blasted a 12-gauge loaded with buckshot. It's uncertain if she hit the beast but she blew out the windows. Both muddy footprints and handprints were found outside the room corroborating the story. Several more terrifying events occurred and the family was forced to simply abandon their home. The events of the Copalis Cowman rarely occur in print but are sewn into the local legend in Grays Harbor County. I had heard the stories myself as locals relayed them to me. Some hypothesize that there were two Sasquatch and the male was the aggressor and the female had a maternal affection to the young boy (Baker).

***

Certain coincidences crept up as I was researching and writing this book. One such serendipitous anomaly was the fact that Herrington and I seemed to share some of the same duty areas, me some 35 years later. My first Ranger residence

Figure 8: Site of Verlin Herrington's encounter.

was on the windy beach at Copalis and I traveled all of the same back roads. I've not been fortunate enough to witness a Sasquatch crossing. Still, though, Copalis is tiny and rural. Our homes couldn't have been separated by more than a mile.

This is one of those happy coincidences that really made me feel like I was on the right track.

There were two events within a month of each other in the year 1970. One sighting in May occurred by way of a nighttime road sighting near Copalis Crossing (M4) and a month later, some 20 miles away, near Tahola there was a sighting spurred by mysterious rock-throwing (Green, The Sasquatch File, p. 52).

There is A LOT of acreage to the peninsula with a diverse array of environments including mountains, rivers, brackish sloughs, saltwater bays, livestock range, farms, rain forests, alpine lakes, sacred native land, ocean battered coastline, and even cranberry bogs! You'd be crazy to explore every Bigfoot haunt the Olympic Peninsula has to offer in one visit…but if you do, let's talk because you're my kind of crazy!

If you're vacationing in or around Ocean Shores then a day trip up to Lake Quinault is probably on your itinerary. There are many things to do along the shores of Lake Quinault and no shortage of outstanding hikes and stunning vistas. It was along the North Shore Road that a postal carrier saw a Sasquatch, snapped an (albeit blurry) cellphone photo and posted his report to the BFRO (BFRO #24379).

The indigenous people of the Quinault Tribe refer to the Say-yat-kah. Kapoeman, a village patriarch in 1969 told a *Seattle Post Intelligencer* reporter that "our people have seen these Say-yat-kah and will see them again." (Place, pp. 117-118).

It's doubtful that Forks' *Twilight* fame will carry their economy into the next decade so why not cruise up to Forks and pump a few bucks into their local economy? Get a chicken fried steak or burger at a local logger café and head out on your hunt![14]

Now let's travel to the eastern side of the Peninsula where fiords and beautiful bays line the Hood Canal and Puget Sound. The communities of Quilcene

---

[14] This is what I would eat. Get what you want.

(oregonbigfoot.com #00782) and Brinnon (M3) have had encounters with our legendary ape-man (BFRO #941).

Figure 9: Elk cross Dosewallips Road.

It's here that I had a strange encounter. While researching this book, I left at sunrise one morning and boarded the ferry at Edmonds on an expedition to investigate Bigfoot haunts along U.S. 101. I was about an hour and a half into my journey when my incessant bladder decided a quick stop was necessary. With no filthy gas station restroom in sight, I stopped along the road south of Quilcene and decided to water the flora. I chose this particular spot hastily because my bladder had told me. Is this the epitome of a gut feeling? I walked a very short distance up a wet mountain road, the fog rising from the asphalt. I was surrounded by lush sword ferns and towering evergreens. I noticed something peculiar upon the road cut. There was an obvious game trail and some small trees that had been snapped over. They stood out because, in my time as a Ranger, I routinely evaluated trees for hazards and cleaned up fallen ones after a storm. I'd kind of become the CSI Ranger when it came to how or why a tree came down and the damage it did on its way. To me, these laid-over saplings seemed unusual…young, healthy trees generally don't fail like this and I couldn't see where a larger tree or limb had caused this damage. I know the peninsula gets snow but rarely is it heavy at the lower elevations and I was but a few feet above sea level. Knowing that hypotheses suggest Sasquatch marks trails in such a manner, I was inclined to check this out. Mind you, this wasn't exactly the "smoking gun" in terms of THE OBVIOUS BIGFOOT EXPLANATION…it had merely piqued my interest. Then I saw a print.

On the incline of the road cut, about four feet from broken trees was a large, foot-shaped depression. It was significantly longer and wider than my size 13 boot. I'd say it was 15 inches in length. Dear readers, hopefully by now, I've earned your trust. While I'm enthusiastic about my Bigfoot exploits I'm neither duplicitous or naïve. I have a bachelor's degree in journalism, I've held a law enforcement commission and I was a Park Ranger for 10 years. I have an investigatory nature. It's going to be up to your internal judge of character as to whether or not you trust my credibility. I'm going to present this information to you fairly and without a great deal of prejudice then, you can decide for yourself whether or not I was literally on the trail of a Sasquatch.

I was looking at something that looked like a huge footprint. It wasn't perfect. It didn't have a perfectly-formed series of five toes like the photos in the books. But it was clearly the impression of something heavy and not a peculiar geological enigma.

Figure 10: Left: unmodified photo of foot-shape depression in ground. Right: Same depression highlighted to show what I interpreted as the shape of a foot. The oval represetns the "big toe on the left foot."

Here's the kicker. I had, within my ability, the means to take detailed measurements and cast the print. I had my freakin' Bigfoot kit in the car! My own personal skepticism somehow browbeat my confidence so much that I'd rather have convinced myself it couldn't be a Sasquatch print than walk 75 feet to the car and get my forensic supplies. I drove away trying to convince myself I hadn't seen what I'd seen. I've yet to come up with another explanation. Fellow Bigfooters, if you see a print, document it to the best of your abilities. Worry about whether or not it *is* or *isn't* after the fact.

When in doubt, cast it!

I even revisited the location (about two weeks later). The tree-breaks made the site easy to find again. But I couldn't relocate the print. Lesson learned. At least I have a photo. I submitted the photo and a report to the BFRO. The researcher that responded felt it was an authentic Bigfoot print.

Exactly 13 months later to the day I attended an expedition arranged by The Olympic Project. A group of Bigfoot researchers known as the Ridgewalkers hosted an investigation and series of demonstrations and lectures from their property nestled neatly between the Olympic National Forest and Olympic National Park. Ridgewalkers' cofounder and Bigfoot documentary veteran, Derek Randles leads tours and expeditions from the Bigfoot basecamp with the help of his wife Torrie and sweet family. This camp is to the Sasquatch enthusiast that Rock and Roll Fantasy Camp is to the aspiring rocker. It provides networking opportunities and a chance to hang out with your heroes.

The best thing I gained that weekend was a friend. I met a man named Scott Robinson. Scott is a writer and blogger. We hit it off immediately, and one evening, while others were out on the Cliff Barackman night hike, we enjoyed a couple of beers by the woodstove in the Bigfoot barracks.[15]

Scott really enjoys learning about the weird side of Bigfoot. He is very intrigued by stories about portals and other strange occurrences. Our mutual interest in Sasquatch, no matter how much our interpretations differed, made us close friends. Scott and I have been in the field together many times.

***

The class was extremely useful to me. One of the things I learned, and admittedly should've known was: There's rarely just one print. It is possible, however, that a creature walking in asphalt would step in mud and leave a single print. Many possibilities like this allow for trail disappearance. A seasoned tracking veteran could no doubt follow the signs but I was certainly unqualified to do so. Still, though, there had to have been more impressions in the duff on the day I had made that discovery.

So, traveling back in time 13 months, I wish I'd searched harder for those subsequent prints or subtle indentations that would constitute a trackway. I looked (admittedly briefly) and found nothing. If I may make an admonishing confession, I felt uncomfortable. The woods atop that road cut may as well have had a witch's cottage built from candy standing amongst the moss-covered snarling trees and twisted limbs. Not ten feet from the paved road stood a picture-

---

[15] It was actually a well-lit barn at the Bigfoot camp, but barracks sounded better.

perfect representation of the deep-dark woods. I stood there and felt the cold dampness of the dark environment consuming me and contemplated walking further in search of more prints. I was overwhelmed with the sensation of being watched. I know this isn't scientific but it's sure a visceral response and hard to overrule when it happens to you. When I noticed I could hear my heart beating, I was startled by how quiet the world around me had become. The woods had fallen silent. No longer did the Towie "schree" or the Stellar's Jay "screrch"…silence. "This is probably private property." I convinced myself. I turned around and walked back to my car. All I have to show for my discovery is one ambiguous photo with no indication of scale. I learned a lesson and, flash forward to Bigfoot bootcamp, looked back on the folly of my ways vowing not to repeat these mistakes.

So, I leave it up to you. But, let's say for a second that it was a print made by a living, breathing Sasquatch. Then, I'm either extremely lucky or these things are walking around all over the place!

It was the Summer of '69!

As mentioned, the late 1960s hit a fever pitch of Sasquatch sightings, documented footprints, and encounters. In the same year Bryan Adam's claims to have purchased his "first real six-string," Bigfoot reports surged from California to British Columbia. So much so that John Green was inspired to pen *Year of the Sasquatch*.

Sharing the Washington accounts, Green listed the following 1969 Bigfoot reports:

-March, Sighting in Skamania County
-March, 18-inch tracks in Skamania County
-April, rancher sees "huge tracks" near Bossburg
-April, four men witness 20-inch tracks with a 5-foot stride
-April, a sighting near Bossburg
-*Spring*, a sighting near Kettle Falls
-July, sighting near Bossburg
-July, Deputy Herrington's sighting, Grays Harbor County
-*Summer*, tracks found near Forks
-August, teenage boys file report with forest rangers claiming to have been chased by "three hairy human-like creatures" at Cub Lake near Darrington
-September, nighttime road crossing north of Deception Pass
-*Fall*, tracks found by Ivan Marx[16]
-October, two Sasquatch seen west of Yakima
-*Fall*, two people report sighting in their yard in Fife
-November, loggers see Bigfoot near Neah Bay

---

[16] Ivan Marx will be mentioned later as his role in Bossburg and the Cripplefoot incident is substantial.

Secretly Seeking Sasquatch

-November, sighting near Colockum Pass, Wenatchee
-November, close sighting and subsequent footprints in Woodland
-November, Bossburg Cripplefoot event gains traction
-December, 17-inch tracks encircle Whistle Lake, Anacortes

This is purely speculative on my part but I don't believe it is careless to state this: I believe the Patterson-Gimlin film ignited most of this firestorm. As I'm sure you're familiar, the film was shot in October of 1967 and records, according to proponents of the footage, an actual Sasquatch female striding hastily away from the men in a remote creek washout at Bluff Creek, California. While always controversial, the film did reach public viewings in 1968. Most of these were done by way of lectures in large venues. In fact, I was told by Dr. Jeff Meldrum himself, that as a youngster he saw the film at the Spokane Coliseum thus igniting his interest in this creature.

Undoubtedly, the sensation that the film generated contributed to 1969's bumper year of Sasquatch encounters. This, however, does not mean they're untrue but the timing cannot be overlooked. I do not believe there were actually *more* Bigfoot encounters with people. There were certainly more *reports*. Bear in mind not all sightings or encounters are *reported*. What does *reported* even mean? Telling someone of authority who'll keep a record, I guess. *Someone of authority*, of course, could be a researcher, a journalist, or a law enforcement officer. I'm not knowledgeable enough in statistics to even wager a guess but I believe I can make a safe assertion that most Bigfoot encounters go unreported. In '69, more reports were filed than ever before. Unfortunately, a report is always fallible.

To simplify the following example, let's assume that these reports are all actual sightings. Any report, looked at through the "did-it-happen-o-meter" is susceptible to the following possibilities:

- The witness is truthful in that they believe they witnessed a Bigfoot but misidentified something else.

-The reporting party is lying thereby perpetuating a hoax that could be accompanied by faked forensic evidence and fraudulent film.

-A witness may believe what they saw but have been hoaxed by another party.

-Lastly, the witness saw a genuine Bigfoot creature and had the courage and confidence to tell someone.

I don't need to remind you that, in '69, there was no internet but it does seem more people were emboldened to report their claims. There were Bigfoot researchers to telephone or write and most of those individuals were dedicated enough to travel to visit the witness. If a single one of these reports is true in the sense of an actual human encounter with the legendary man-ape, then, that is important beyond any quantifiable reckoning.

The Northern Cascades

Likely too early to have been influenced by the Patterson-Gimlin film, in 1967 folks living along the Nooksack River in the shadow of Mount Baker (M6) had their own streak of eerie encounters (Green, The Best of Bigfoot Sasquatch, p. 137).

Follow the water. There are some enticing encounters from the region surrounding Mount Baker. The Nooksack River produced a ton of reports in the '60s. It's not surprising when you consider that the river is undammed and provides an unencumbered thoroughfare for spawning salmon. Speculatively it would seem to provide a valuable feeding corridor for Bigfoot as well.

Going back in time is an intriguing account. In 1946 Mrs. Chapman hurriedly gathered her children and fled as a Sasquatch strode purposely toward their Ruby Creek domicile. That evening, her startled husband returned home to find a shed ransacked and salmon barrels overturned and raided. He later found his family safe but frightened in town. The family abandoned their property (Napier, Bigfoot: The Yeti and Sasquatch in Myth and Reality, pp. 80-81). Ruby Creek is near Chilliwack B.C. Ruby Creek proper flows into Ross Lake (reservoir) which straddles the U.S./Canadian border. There are Bigfoot reports abound on the waterways surrounding Mount Baker, Ruby Mountain, and Shuksan. Campers, hunters, hikers, and even ranchers report encounters near Baker Lake. There's even a Devil's Creek[17] to add to the eeriness and mystique.

Figure 11: The Mount Baker drive in the fall. My apologies if you're viewing this in black and white.

This won't be the first-time serendipity is mentioned in this book. Through much of what I considered to be the academic side of the research, I read, very nearly, every Bigfoot book and watched and re-watched every Bigfoot documentary I could find. On several episodes of Monsterquest, I was quite enamored with the exploits of one Adam Davies (pronounced Davis). He was the real deal…he has searched for Yeti in the Himalayas and the Mokele-Mbembe (pronounced Mbembe) in the Congo. His Monsterquest pursuits involved the Yeti, the Chinese Wildman, and The Orang Pendek. The latter, in my opinion, will be the first bipedal cryptid to be documented and recognized by science. It is likely a cousin to our Orangutan and learned bipedalism in its tropical, volcano-ridden Sumatran climate.

I respect Adam's determination, intelligence, and scientific approach. This led me to read *Man Beasts: A Personal Investigation*, a book penned by Davies. I enjoyed the book thoroughly. In particular, I enjoyed his telling of adventures, misadventures, and tales of friends and enemies he made along the way. This book, the one you're reading, could've been a matter-of-fact guidebook with the text serving mainly to introduce you to the maps. *Man Beasts* was confirmation to

---

[17] The historical tendency to name Bigfoot haunts after the devil and other evil manifestations is discussed in the "An Ape by any other Name" chapter.

me that it was okay to tell the personal story and even embarrassing mistakes or occurrences. Adam, who at the time resided in England, and I struck up a friendship via Facebook where I revealed to him, I had actually been conducting a great deal of my research in areas he wrote about in *Man Beasts*. While he was more than amicable concerning my efforts, he suggested I contact Lori Simmons who had worked the area very thoroughly carrying on her father's research. Lori has a very specific area she is researching. This area in the Northern Cascades is rife with Sasquatch activity. Correspondence with Lori led to another new friend. She lived locally, and we shared many adventures. In my opinion, this area *belongs* to her. It raised an interesting conundrum: if you do this long enough, you're bound to cross paths with another Bigfooter. Likely it may be someone who has staked a very personal claim to the area. Encroaching on their land (we speak of public land here, of course, not private property) could feel like poaching in a way. For one thing, it's public land and this is America…so long as what you're doing is legal, no one can tell you not to poke around for Bigfoot in any certain area. On the other hand, I hope you feel compelled to execute discretion and even reach out to a fellow researcher should the opportunity arise. There may be an opportunity for collaboration. Either way, should you begin investigating, I suggest you practice discretion and contact fellow researchers when you can and when you feel your "area" overlaps.

Lori will always credit the dedicated work of her departed father, Donald Wallace. Wallace was a true mountain man, a hunter, and trapper who later in life fell into the Bigfootverse after a series of strange encounters in the Northern Cascades. Most of Lori's first book consists of his journal investigating "The Big Guy," a rambunctious noise-maker that Wallace believed spent most of the daylight underground in some sort of tree-root-cave, a *den* of sorts. Most of Lori's work centers around documenting the truly alarming noises that can be recorded in the Wallace/Simmons research area.

The most alarming event I've had while investigating the Sasquatch happened one day, alone, near the purported den. I heard concussive booms which seemed to emanate from underground and were quite unnerving. I don't know if what I heard was a Sasquatch but the sound was eerie, resonated in my chest, and felt as though it was caused by something sentient. There is an inherent danger in anthropomorphizing such occurrences. Nonetheless, I was shaken by the events that day and still don't know what to make of it.

Essentially, I decided to move my personal pursuits away from Lori's hot spot and into the woods and rivers surrounding Darrington and Oso (M7). The Sasquatch are there. I hope Lori gets the proof she is looking for. Her journey is very personal. Far more personal than mine. You can read about her journey in *Tracking Bigfoot* and *Tracking Bigfoot: The Journey Continues*.

This area is wonderful and about 2 hours from my house. The four-hour roundtrip drive, much of which is on a dusty mountain road is EXHAUSTING, I won't lie. I do however believe that if I'm able to document good forensic or photographic evidence, it will be in this section of the Northern Cascades.

Figure 12: Moss-draped tree in northern Cascades.

***

In June of 2000, 16-inch giant bare footprints were found along the "Mountain Loop Highway" (Coleman, Bigfoot!: The True Story of Apes in America, p. 13). Explore the Mountain Loop Highway (M7) for unparalleled views and a better-than-average shot at seeing this man-beast!

Southwest Washington

I was fortunate enough to have been invited onto private property near native Chehalis land in southwestern Washington. I accompanied Adam Davies and his then-fiancé, now wife, Nadia Moore. Nadia is an Immunocellular Laboratory Research Associate. Combined with Adam's experience and resume', we (at least *they*) brought a lot of credibility to this investigation.

Figure 13: Adam Davies

The month was July. It was hot. Traffic sucked. The couple and I traversed the slog of Interstate 5 and met up with a wonderful woman and her family.

The family had been having Sasquatch problems. I can't go into too much detail because I believe it is imperative to protect the privacy of the witnesses and the sanctity of the location. Suffice to say, their home bordered farmland and a river which flowed right out of the woods of Bigfootville, USA (my term). The family had become quite unnerved by nighttime visitors that prowled around somewhat regularly and, on more than one occasion, left coyote viscera high in the tree limbs, a gesture that simultaneously seems like a gift and a warning.

Our hostess was delightfully hospitable and was eager to give us a tour of the property and share some of the happenings.

We set up our tents in the cow pasture where most of the activity and a sighting had occurred. Now when I say it was 105 degrees Fahrenheit, I want you to understand that I'm exaggerating. It was 102 degrees that day. Not fully comprehending how long we'd be away from camp; we followed our guide into the brush without a single drop of water. Making matters worse, Adam had asked me to bring a jar of jam. He wanted to conduct an experiment where, on a paper plate with some ultra-sticky double-stick tape with the jam as a tasty bait, the tape, hopefully, would collect hairs from the sweet-toothed creature. With any luck, those hairs would be from a Sasquatch and contain that all-important follicle and yield DNA.

I could've simply grabbed a couple of McDonald's packets of jelly from the junk drawer back home but I opted to bring marmalade. Why marmalade? My family had just seen *Paddington Bear* the "live-action" film released in 2014. Thinking my children would enjoy the taste of marmalade, the way Paddington does, I bought a jar and hoped to earn some hero-dad status for such a literal movie treat tie-in (we're big into those). It turns out marmalade is awful. It is bitter and…um…bitter. It is like gelatin made from orange peels. So, wishing to get rid of this but not wholly waste it, I decided it would be adequate Bigfoot bait. Certainly, the bears would enjoy it.

It was a substantial jar of marmalade and glass with a metal lid. I placed the twenty-eight-ounce jar in the cargo pocket of my cotton shorts on this hot summer day. "Adam, should I bring the marmalade?" I asked.

"Yes Jason, do. We may find a good area to set our trap," was Adam's response in his charming British accent.

So, through the pasture, and the tall grass, and the parched river banks we explored what, essentially consisted of, the acreage between I-5 and the Pacific Ocean. Some men are prone to chafing and some aren't. Even the men who never chafe will chafe occasionally. To say I chafed that day does not give tribute to the severity of discomfort the infirmity can produce. The kicker is, a point I will never forget, the marmalade was not deployed in any way during this two-hour death hike. It traveled in my cargo shorts, swinging against my skin and weighing me down.

By the time we returned to the house we were filthy, sweaty, thirsty and without hyperbole, in the early stages of heat exhaustion. Our hostess showed no ill-effects. Her home was air-conditioned and she cooked dinner for us and we drank copious amounts of precious ice water.

Adam, Nadia, and I devised a plan for the time remaining between dinner and dusk and how we would conduct our night investigation. We set the marmalade trap. We set up trail cams and we even recovered a hair sample from where our hostess said the creature crosses a barbed-wire fence. I limped through the chaffing discomfort as best I could and it wasn't long before we were enjoying cold drinks and company around their backyard fire pit. The host, the husband, and father of the family arrived home after dark. He immediately struck me as an extremely intelligent and observant man. He added his experiences to the Bigfoot conundrum they were facing. He and another witness had seen the creature. He described it and, what was interesting, described a feeling of disgust. He said, "it looked gross." He is a very articulate man, but it was clear he was struggling to describe how he felt when he actually faced the creature. Searching for the words he erred on the side of simplicity.

That night was an interesting one for me. We enjoyed our drinks well past midnight and as the sky grew darker and darker the stories came out. Let's call them "ghost stories" but most were of the Bigfoot variety. I remained mostly silent, listening and taking it all in. Adam and Nadia, through years of experience with the Bigfoot community and in the field (most of which happened before they met), regaled the group with their personal tales and those they had heard from others. The most disturbing things I heard that night involved *other things* happening in places, usually at night, that didn't have anything to do with Bigfoot and were much scarier. This is when I was introduced to the *rabbit hole*.

After a short night hike, we returned to our tents. To my relief, no one in the group ripped on me too badly for admitting my rather personal chafing problem. A lot of walking simply wasn't in the cards for me. The stories that night haunted me and I felt foolishly nervous like a child. Two stories stuck in my mind: a female apparition taunting one group of researchers (only two of the three could see her) and a dogman-like creature witnessed by a Park Ranger who, having been caught out on the trail way too late, admitted he was lucky to be alive.

To me these are just stories. I cannot confirm any sort of credibility to the witnesses because, by the time they reached my ears, they were third party hearsay. That didn't make them any less scary that night alone in my tent and grappling to understand how I could allow for these paranormal occurrences in a world where I was determined to only consider a Bigfoot of flesh and blood. On this night the nature of my book changed. I could not now wholly rule out the a-little-too-weird occurrences in certain places. These were places where Bigfoot also seemed to reside. Conversely, I cannot accept every account of other-than-earthly occurrences as canon. My mind was cluttered with more questions concerning the land of Sasquatch than ever before and boyhood memories, nearly lost, crept back into my consciousness concerning my strange relationship with Rock Lake and my grandparents' home. The chapter: Wired for Weird will address this conundrum in greater detail.

The jury is still out on the recovered hair sample. While on the death hike, at the very edge of my hearing, I heard a forlorn howl. I can't rule out a canine source but it sounded like how you'd expect a Sasquatch to sound (admittedly a fallacy listed in Arment's book). Our hostess heard it too. She said "did you hear that? That's that red [bastard]." Each of our hosts reported the Bigfoot was red in color like an orangutan.

We survived the night. Adam, Nadia, and I departed our hosts with hugs and headed to Lake Cushman for relaxation and recovery. It was very nice to soak in the reservoir's cool, not cold, water and listen at night for Bigfoot calls and depart on leisurely excursions up forest service roads.

Figure 14: An idyllic summer evening near Lake Cushman.

***

In *Where Bigfoot Walks: Crossing the Dark Divide*, naturalist Robert Michael Pyle pens a type of memoir about his experiences looking for Bigfoot. It's written in a transcendental style similar to Henry David Thoreau with a touch of John Muir.

He debates what Sasquatch's home and range may be and specifically whether or not the creature could succeed in second-growth forests, meaning, lands that have been logged and are now covered with a second forest of trees (by this time, truthfully, much of Washington's Forest Service land is now third growth). I pondered this question at great length on my trips to coastal Washington. Initially, as I drove through the clear cuts, I felt that previously-disturbed lands were like a nest in which a bird refused to return. Does a wild animal like Bigfoot only exist in the wilderness and old-growth or could he return to lands indelibly altered by man? (Pyle, 2017)

Consider this: deer, elk, coyote, cougar, and bear have all returned. Most of the forest animals found a way to adapt. In fact, the elk historically had been a plains animal but were pushed into the forests as man's reach, and appetite for elk meat, increased. I'm not saying this is ideal but I'm not going to take a shot at the logging industry here. My house was made from wood and I use, quite regularly, toilet paper. With any luck, this book's pages are paper. I don't wish to take this for granted. I can simply say that for recreation and respite, I prefer wilderness and old-growth but we're fortunate to have second and third growth forests. Furthermore, logging in the U.S. simply isn't conducted like it was 100 years ago. It's far from ideal, but so long as the area provides food, water, and the type of cover organisms need, most of them will return. In this sense, anecdotal evidence, along with physical evidence, the best of which is footprints, suggest that Bigfoot has indeed returned to areas disturbed by the expansion of man. There are still things to eat, water to drink, and places to hide.

Bigfoot has been seen by loggers. The creature has been witnessed striding across a clear-cut, crossing second (or third) growth forest roads, haunting private tree farms and even peering into windows of homes (Bord, p. 32). To quote Ian Malcolm (Jeff Goldblum, *Jurassic Park*), it would seem, "life finds a way."

The areas southwest of Olympia haven't produced a prolific number of reports like the peninsula and Grays Harbor County to the north but the handful of reports from the region seem to be really good ones. In the sixties, when Deputy Herrington was reeling from his encounter on DeKay Road, footprints were popping up in areas south of WA 8 in the Capitol Forest. It was here, I found a nice and surprisingly beautiful drive into the heart of southwest Washington's Bigfoot country.

Figure 15: A shady and cool spot in the Capitol Forest.

"Before the white people came to this country, a big Skookum, or hairy man, came and drove all the Indians away that were living on the Pe Ell Prairie and the Indians never went back there to live..." Green cites *Told by the Pioneers*[18] in this telling of a Skookum scaring the indigenous away from Pe Ell (Green, Sasquatch: The Apes Among Us, p. 25).

Another account stirs from Grays Harbor County, this time in the woods south of Elma and the areas surrounding the Satsop River and Oakville (M7). Deputy Dennis Heryford was already a seasoned Bigfoot veteran by the time he was called to investigate strange tracks in 1982 (Guttilla, pp. 247-248). As a boy growing up near Elma, he reports he had seen an 8-foot-tall hairy creature jump from a tree as he returned home from school. He got a good look at it and sprinted toward the safety of his house. He stopped to look back and saw the

---

[18] I tried to reference *Told by the Pioneers* directly but was unable to obtain the correct volume and Green did not include a page number.

hairy creature running just as expediently away from the boy, on two legs and swinging its arms with every step (McGauley, 1984).

So, it is fitting that Heryford, along with two other deputies were involved with documenting strange trackways of large individuals with footprints measuring 15 and 17 inches. Heryford kept a Bigfoot File and poured casts of some of the tracks (see Figure 16). The full police report can be found on the BFRO's website (report #2599).

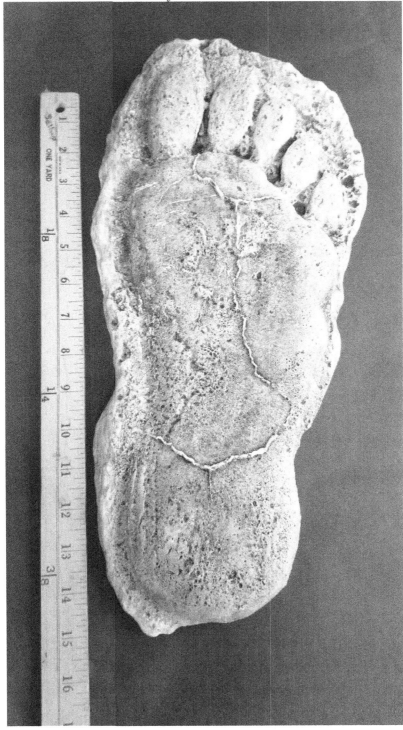

Figure 16: A copy of the Heryford cast from the Meldrum Collection.

If you connected the dots from activity reported in or near the towns of Raymond, Artic (sic), Oakville, Doty, Pe Ell (M9), and the Chehalis Indian Reservation, and taking into consideration the Chehalis River, you get a web and the spider resides within the Capitol Forest (M8). Your most logical access point is Capitol Forest Road (2.5 miles north, northwest of Oakville on US 12). This is DNR land (Washington State Department of Natural Resources), a sister agency of my Washington State Parks. And, like Washington State Parks, you'll need a "Discover Pass" for your vehicle to access the lands (as of 2018). At this time, the pass is either $10/day or $30/year. Please purchase your pass ahead of time and review any laws and regulations concerning public lands.

I drove the road on the Saturday of Labor Day Weekend. It was surprisingly tame. I saw but a handful of campers and one man preparing to do some shooting practice at a rock pit. It occurs to me that you'd share this road with busy logging trucks on workdays. I was quite taken aback, however, by how wild and untamed this area of the forest seemed. You can still catch glimpses of clear cuts and much of the area is visibly divvied up to logging contracts but here there is still an eerie presence.

Figure 17: The sun breaks through in the Capitol Forest.

Jason M. Burke

Over the River and Through the Wood

Have you ever seen a baby pigeon? Well, neither have I. I got a hunch they exist.

-Dr. Wallace Wrightwood (Don Ameche), 'Harry and the Hendersons' (Amblin Entertainment).

Chances are, if you live in Washington, a trek across the mountains is not foreign to you. Most motorists will hop on I-90 and try to burn up much real estate as they can, all the while thinking: "boy the middle of the state is very, VERY boring." I've traversed this route a lot and Snoqualmie Pass (on Interstate 90) to me, is just as boring as the middle of the state. Seriously, I've come to think of the Seattle/Spokane trip as a burden and the most interesting parts are my *nearly* favorite Starbucks in Ellensburg or convincing your kids to play "count the windmills" to pass the time. There are, however, much more scenic ways to cross the Cascade Mountain Range in Washington.

Figure 18: Welcome to Sasquatch Country.

I felt it would be a cop-out to include each of the mountain passes as an individual Sasquatch route. I decided to evaluate them on their own merit and list the top contenders here. US 12 (White Pass) does have a rich Bigfoot history but it lacked the scenic qualities that I thought were important for inclusion in this book (not to worry, US 12 will still make it into this guide). Interstate 90 was out of the question because chances are, you've already traversed it or will at some point in your life. I was blown away by WA 410, though. 410 essentially connects Yakima to Enumclaw. It cuts through the Cascades with Cayuse and Chinook Pass and, at times, offers a little white-knuckle driving. All of a sudden: BAM! Mount Rainier hits you like the 14,410-foot stratovolcano it is. Amazing views and ample wildlife, WA 410 gets my thumbs up, three Sasquatch, four-star rating. Reports of encounters with the hairy giant are spread from Naches to Greenwater (M15) and a roadside store sells trinkets and asks you to submit your Bigfoot reports in their guestbook. Campers have reported sightings and strange noises. Bumping Lake (M15) has been a hotbed for such activity (BFRO reports #1462, 3368, 382 et al). So many strange noises have been reported at Bumping Lake it makes me wonder how exactly that lake got its name. Recent reports claim prints were found near Snoquera (BFRO #1594).

Figure 19: Further confirmation: You're in Bigfoot Country.

Another immeasurable option is U.S. 2/Steven's Pass. Known as Washington's Alps, the Cascades jut up out of the quaint Bavarianeque town of Leavenworth (M16) with impossible beauty and grandeur. There are plenty of cozy places to stay and there is never a shortage of cold Austrian ales or warm German potato salad. Sasquatch has stomped around this region for decades and has been seen on or around Highway 2. The area is so famous for Sasquatch lore that the *Harry and the Hendersons* film crew shot some of the movie's scenes near Index and some aspects of the set remain. In the film, Don Ameche plays Dr. Wallace Wrightwood. The character is an amalgam of Bigfoot researchers made famous by their books and adventures from preceding decades (Cliff Crook, in particular). Bigfoot buffs have noticed pieces of John Green and Dr. Grover Krantz (Coleman, The Origins of Dr. Wallace Wrightwood, Jacques LaFleur and Harry of Harry and the Hendersons, 2013).

At the summit of Stevens pass is the community of Index (M16). Here you'll find ample Bigfoot photo-ops and even Dr. Wrightwood's research center which was featured in the film.

Now...I don't, for a second, present this as the gospel. But a story was relayed to me about the filming of *Harry and the Hendersons*. The story goes that a Forest Service employee (described as a Ranger in the narrative I heard) was overseeing the day's filming sitting in his truck to stop traffic. He became suddenly and rather sheepishly aware that he may have inadvertently parked his vehicle in the shot. He thought this because Bigfoot very deliberately walked out of the woods and crossed the road in front of him. So, he moved his truck. While discussing his gaffe with the film crew, he was shocked to find that the crew vehemently denied working where the employee claimed, let alone anyone in a Sasquatch costume. Certainly, there's a cautious grain of salt to take with this story lest one be completely gullible. Perhaps it could be filed in the urban legend category along with the curtain ghost in *Three Men and a Baby* but it's a fun tale to share nonetheless.

If you're spending time in or near Yakima (M14), the obvious choice is to head out on a loop through the southern Cascades. BFRO Report #26065 shares a road crossing on a gravel road near WA 410 and #1686 retells a riverside sighting from US 12 (M14).

Elk hunters experienced a frightful howl while camping near Rimrock Lake. The creature was close and shrieked as the hunters tried to illuminate it with a spotlight. The creature slinked away unseen but the noise it let out reportedly woke up other campers (BFRO #3759). Bumping Lake persists as being a hotspot. It was relayed to me that Bob Gimlin (one-third of the participants in the Patterson Gimlin Film[19]), now 86 years old, wished to camp at Bumping Lake for an opportunity to see the beast one more time. Footprints have been found around the lake.

---

[19] Roger Patterson and Patty the Sasquatch being the other two.

Figure 20: Photo op! Harry Henderson at the town of Index.

The Skookums of Skamania County

Years ago, when I was a Ranger in-training and as green as my ranger trousers, I took a work-related trip to Beacon Rock State Park. I was one of the two Rangers-in-training at Ocean City State Park. This was in the Southwest Region, by State Parks' designation. All new rangers in the region were required to attend a mandatory orientation. This was presented by way of a day-long class hosted by Beacon Rock State Park just outside the city of Vancouver, WA. Our park manager made sure that Jesse, the other new Ranger at my park, and I knew that we were required to go. Jesse had transplanted from Rochester, New York in pursuit of his ranger career, and I had moved across the state. Both being VERY new and away from home, we quickly bonded and became very good friends. I felt comforted by knowing Jesse would share this ordeal with me.

Jesse did not go. Apparently, "required" and "mandatory," by Jesse's definition were still negotiable terms. So, I made the trek alone. It's a pretty hearty drive from Ocean Shores to Beacon Rock. SW Region staff informed participants that they could arrive the night before and "camp out" so as to be ready for the 8 a.m. start time of the orientation. This is what I chose to do. What I expected was to meet some other new rangers who were thrust into the same predicament as me, enjoy some beer, and hit the hay. This was not meant to be. I arrived, after dark, to find three people, the region manager (my boss's boss), the assistant region manager (my boss's supervisor) and the region's secretary. They were extremely friendly and accommodating though, and Paul, the region's manager, as it turns out, was a fan of fine microbrews. Each of them had their own camper to retire to. I did not. I brought a tent and it was starting to rain. When I describe the rain as a shower, I want you to fully understand my meaning. I don't mean a *shower* in the sense of a passing rain spritz. I mean, I may as well have set up the tent in a running bathroom shower. It was a miserable, soaking rain and anything touching the tent walls was getting wet.

My mind mulled over my options. I didn't feel I could knock on any of the camper doors. I wasn't comfortable with that. There were a few Adirondacks nearby. These are 3-sided wooden structures with a roof and built-in bunks. They offer about as much protection from the elements as do the wooden lounge chairs of the same name. The bunks were essentially wooden shelves meant for you to bring your own mattress. I wasn't exactly fond of the idea of sleeping in the Adirondack with the entire front of the shelter exposed to the weather and creepy woods and the possibility of a Sasquatch sneaking in and peacefully watching me sleep, lovingly brushing my cheek like some even creepier version of Boo Radley. My best, spur-of-the-moment solution was to move my tent inside the shelter and set it up on the floor. At least it would be drier. Exhausted, damp, and uncomfortable, I laid down in my new bivouac. It wasn't long before I heard "thap…thap…thap…" Pause. "Thap…thap thap…thap." The Adirondack's roof leaked! It was maddening. Many a camper has claimed that hearing the rain patter against the rainfly is as relaxing as any lullaby. This was not the case here. There was no "white-noise" quality to this drip. It was like a child bouncing marble after marble onto a snare drum.

I won't bore you with the details of my successive impromptu solutions that I frantically enacted well into that dark rainy night. Where I ended up was in the passenger seat of my state parks' Sonoma. It was an extremely sleepless and uncomfortable night and I'm pretty sure I have a permanent number 9 stamped-into my hip where it rested too long against the dial on the police radio. This was my introduction to Skamania County.

***

Figure 21: Two wood apes stand sentinel in Carson.

I departed my hotel room on December 31, 2012, on my inaugural trek into the field for this book. My family, warm and asleep in our room at Skamania Lodge barely stirred when I stepped out into the freezing cold snowstorm. I began to question my sanity and whether or not this whole endeavor was worthwhile. I cruised up WA 141 as the sun crept up and everything came into focus when I was treated to this view (see figure 22). I had received confirmation that this endeavor was worthwhile. A picturesque Mount Adams rested heavily atop the cold and snowy landscape as I drove warm and happy in the car.

This, being my first expedition, was fraught with poor planning and misfortune. It was difficult for me to know exactly which roads would be passable in the middle of winter. I had intended to cruise north, out of White Salmon on WA 141 and then cut over to Wind River Road which is another substantial north-south thoroughfare. But alas, as my tires left the pavement and the snow became deeper, I found a road closure, by way of a 15-foot wall of snow, effectively closing the road to everything but snowmobiles and snowshoes. I did some poking around but surely a thorough investigation into Skamania County and the southern slopes of old Saint Helens would have to wait until summer.

The summer of 2013 was busy with Bigfoot investigations but it took me until November to find the time to schedule the second Skamania expedition. So, with Groupon in-hand my family and I returned to Skamania Lodge in Stevenson, and I departed early on a Saturday morning for the hills.

This time I approached from Wind River Road. It was my intent to drive the mountain roads in as close proximity as I could to reported sightings, and most importantly, Skookum Meadow.

Skookum Meadow is the site of one of the best pieces of Sasquatch forensic evidence. In September of 2000, researchers on a BFRO expedition baited a mud waller with apples. The next day, along with impressions from other animals, it appeared a large beast had laid down to reach for fruit. What's more, the shape, size, and presence of a large heel print with an Achilles tendon suggest this wasn't a mere elk. Copious amounts of plaster were poured and the resulting cast has been studied by many experts willing to go give it their time. Meldrum, as he was part of the initial investigation, has documented this very well in *Where Legend Meets Science* (Meldrum, p. 1899).

So, I made it there. I just didn't plant my flag, so to say. Any desire of mine to get out of the car and walk around was subdued by the well-represented presence of elk hunters. This is by no means an editorial on the elk hunters' collective identification and shooting skills, I just didn't want to get shot. Walking around in the woods that day wasn't a good idea.

Figure 22: A cold, early morning with Mount Adams.

***

Secretly Seeking Sasquatch

The aforementioned Beacon Rock and all the way upriver on WA 14 to White Salmon, have had Sasquatch road crossings. Some of these are even discussed on *In Search Of* in season one, episode five (Landsburg, 1977).

A road crossing has been reported on WA 14 near Stevenson and Sasquatch was sighted near Bear Creek north of Carson on Wind River Road, a drivable route in this book's map section (Green, Year of the Sasquatch, pp. 25-26). In short, Skamania County is one of the best Sasquatch sightings regions in the state.

Jason M. Burke

An Ape by any other Name

Sasquatch. Bigfoot. Oh-ma. Yeti. Momo. Bukwas[20], Harry Henderson. Wooly Bugger. Big Ben. (Guttilla, 2003). These are but a few names used to describe a large hair-covered wildman that has seemingly been in parts of North America as long as indigenous man.

As I've shared with you, my strategy for this book was to assemble a guide by cross-referencing available reports with a map and organizing it in a fashion that is useful and fun to you. In doing so, I poured over pages and pages of my atlas for hours. An *atlas,* and this is for the *younger generation,* is like an analog GPS unit made from paper. It wasn't long before I started to notice trends. For one thing, there are an exorbitant amount of matter-of-fact place names in Washington State. Huckleberry Mountain, Fish Lake, and Elk Meadows to name a few. Remember Rock Lake?

---

[20] It was only in September of 2017, while attending the International Bigfoot Conference that I learned that Bukwas (Bakwas is an alternative spelling), according to First Nations "Kwakiutl" people, is this creature King of Ghosts, much smaller than a Sasquatch who tempts people to eat ghost food and beckons wanderers to drown in order to capture their soul. I learned this from Thomas Sewid, of the aforementioned Kwakiutl tribe. He claimed to stop reading any Bigfoot book which likened Sasquatch to the Bukwas. So dear Thomas, Read on!

Figure 23: Bak'was a native spirit believed by costal natives as the "wildman of the woods." Mask at the Burke Museum, Seattle.

Skookum is a word born of Chinook Jargon. Chinook Jargon is a sort of common tongue among west coast tribes to aid in communication and trading where languages differed. This slang dialect proved useful to Europeans trading with the natives and the language grew to encompass French and English words.

Skookum means "strong." It is also a type of Indian Doll. But, more importantly to our usage, it was used to describe an evil spirit and a hirsute wild man to be avoided in the Pacific wilderness (Meldrum, p. 1901). As I looked over my maps, Skookum appeared repeatedly. Several regional hotspots I plotted had some sort of *Skookum* place name. Skookum Falls, Skookum Creek, Skookum Flats[21], and Skookum Meadow have all had some sort of Bigfoot activity reported. Most self-respecting Bigfoot fans should be familiar with The Skookum Cast, recovered from Skookum Meadow in Skamania County, which is the plaster cast of a suspected Skookum's sacrum. Skookum, Skookum, Skookum. Mere coincidence?

`I thought I had stumbled upon this apparent link between Skookum place

Figure 24: Don't be surprised if you run into a few Skookums in your journeys (WA 410).

names and Bigfoot activity. Then I read Dr. Meldrum's book. Jeff Meldrum Ph.D. is an Associate Professor of Anatomy and Anthropology at Idaho State University. He is well known in the Bigfoot world for his objective and scientific approach to Sasquatch. He has appeared on numerous television specials and

---

[21] NOT the name of a country band.

documentaries and in his book, *Sasquatch: Where Legend Meets Science*, he makes the Skookum place name connection. When I read this, I excitedly told my wife that Dr. Meldrum had just confirmed my findings (seven years earlier, mind you). I was equal parts excited and disappointed. On the one hand, I felt vindicated that my process was legitimate. On the other hand, I wasn't the first to suggest this connection. I hadn't really "discovered" anything. To which my wife replied "You did discover it, sweetie. The same way Columbus discovered America." Thanks, Nicole.

Much to Washington State's credit and charm, settlers retained the Native American place-names albeit many misspelled and/or mispronounced variants. In fact, the term "Sasquatch" is one of these amalgamated variants. The name derives from *sésquac*, from Coastal Salish Tribes of Vancouver, BC (Meldrum, p. 726).

The town of Enumclaw, much of which is farmland carved into the wilds near Mount Rainier, owes its name to natives describing the evil spirits they encountered. Spirits or Sasquatch? Yacolt, near the Bigfoot stronghold of Mount Saint Helens, is known by the natives as a "haunted place" where the spirits abduct children.

As Christians moved here, the word "Devil" begins popping up, many times dovetailing on the eerie phenomena and spirits the indigenous peoples were troubled by. Historically, Sasquatch were commonly referred to as Mountain Devils. I wrote that I found what I believe to be a Sasquatch print near Quilcene. Less than two miles from where I found the print is Devil's Lake.

Settlers were also very practical in place-naming. Being practical in the naming of geologic features and the local geography often outweighed the need to be creative, ironic, or sentimental. So among the Trout Creeks and Dead Horse Gulches, I started to wonder if places like Angry Mountain, Little Giant Pass, Spirit Lake, and Big Devil Peak, all in Bigfoot country, could have forgotten roots in Sasquatch folklore. Which brings us to the strange case of Ape Canyon.

Jason M. Burke

Thar Be Mountain Devils Here!

The best laid plans of mice and men often go awry.

-Robert Burns

The prospectors' cabin was dark and choked by summer heat and the smell of spent gunpowder as five men panicked inside while the mountain devils rained rocks down upon the walls and roof. The beasts that struck blow after blow upon their shack weren't human nor were they fully ape. It was clear to the men though; this assault was about retribution.

That night in July of 1924, Marion Smith, Roy Smith, Gabe Lafever, and Fred Beck witnessed something simultaneously terrifying and extraordinary.

This tale is a staple in Sasquatch lore and stands easily as Washington's most famous Bigfoot story. It's mentioned in virtually every Sasquatch book you'll read. I'll opt on the side of brevity.

In 1924 five men set out from Kelso to revisit their mining claim on Pumy Butte and the Muddy River. You see, the canyon wasn't named "Ape Canyon" yet (Coleman, Bigfoot! The True Story of Apes in America, p. 47). The men rode in a Ford most of the way and then had to walk the rest of the way to their mining claim.[22]

On previous excursions, the men had found human-like footprints around their meager shack and a nearby spring. Natives had long since warned of the

---

[22] I've yet to uncover how many miles needed to be walked and the type of terrain. This seems to be important given the hastiness of their retreat.

mountain devils that resided there but having only seen tracks, the men weren't concerned enough to abandon their mining claim. This all changed that fateful July day. As the story goes, while gathering water from the spring, Marion Smith saw a seven-foot-tall hairy creature watching from behind a tree. Already on edge from eerie noises that preceded this encounter (strange whistles and drum-like concussive sounds), Smith quickly raised and fired 3 successive rounds from his rifle. Roy Smith, Marion's son witnessed the event and agreed that bark sprayed off the tree from bullets whizzing right at the creature's face. Smith maintained that he had to have hit the mystery animal (Green, Sasquatch: The Apes Among Us, p. 92).

The two men rushed back to the cabin and informed the other men as to what had happened. It was late in the day and the group, thoroughly unnerved, agreed to abandon the site. They wouldn't reach the automobile by nightfall and the seemingly safest and most sane option was to stay the night in the cabin.

Best laid plans…

Sometime around midnight, this all went to hell. The creatures they'd witnessed encircled the cabin. They pounded on the walls and threw rocks. There was a hole cut in the cabin's roof, the most primitive of chimneys, and rocks rained through the hole as well. In response, the men fired their guns through the roof and any available holes in the chinking where they may be able to strike their attackers. During the attack, one of the creatures reached through a large hole in the cabin's wall and grabbed an ax. Smith's quick thinking inspired him to turn the ax sideways thus preventing the Sasquatch from acquiring a weapon[23] (Green, Sasquatch: The Apes Among Us, p. 95).

The idea of a 7-foot ax-wielding gorilla is equal parts incredible and terrifying.

The story ends with the ape-men dispatching at dawn and the human men hurriedly departing, leaving all of their tools and abandoning their mining claim. The story goes that they got one more glimpse at a single ape antagonist, standing atop the bluff. In a seemingly amazing cowboy move, Fred Beck took three shots and the creature toppled from the bluff and 400 feet into the river valley below.

The group agreed to keep the traumatizing event a secret…right up until Marion met the first park ranger, on the way home, where he relayed the entire night's events. Back in Kelso, after a few friends were included into the secret, the story leaked to the press and ape mania descended on the small logging town. Newspapers from Portland to Seattle ran the story and bona fide ape hunters

---

[23] Green printed an interview between Roger Patterson and Fred Beck from which most of this story is relayed by this author.

descended on the town. To my knowledge, no apes were tagged and bagged during the chaos.

A very thorough telling of these events appears in *The Bigfoot Classics:* "I Fought the Apemen of Mout St. Helens, WA." The web article is a printing of a piece written by Ronald A. Beck, Fred's son (www.bigfootencounters.com, n.d.).

***

Today, the interpretive bulletin board at Ape Cave, the world's longest lava tube, reads as follows:

What's in a name?

This Lava tube was discovered by Lawrence Johnson in 1951 when he nearly drove a tractor into the main entrance. Lawrence told his friend Harry Reese about his find. Harry and his three sons came early the following year and were the first known explorers of the lava tube. The Reese Boys were members of the St. Helens Apes, a local outdoors club, and led many visitors through the lava tube during the 1950s. The lava tube was named to honor these pioneers.

Concerning the cave, as far as the U.S. Forest Service is concerned, this is where the story ends. There's not a lot of information out there that will pin the name "Apes" on creatures of the simian nature. I don't believe Sasquatch ever inhabited this lava tube but the naming of the boys' club is highly dubious. Ape Canyon is just up the road.

Ape Canyon is, without a doubt, named after the events which unfolded in 1924, whether fact or fiction. THAT my friends is, *What's in a Name*.

Jason M. Burke

Mount Saint Helens Part 2
This Time it's Personal

Getting to Skamania County wasn't the problem. I managed this on several occasions. Getting to Mount Saint Helens, though, seemed to be fraught with hurdles both personal and logistical.

It's necessary to share some of the challenges I've faced so, if anything, you'll have an idea of all the blood, sweat, and tears that went into this process (figuratively and literally). First off, in the late Summer, I learned it was an abominable time to go Bigfooting in roughly 75% of the state. It was all on fire! Almost every time I scheduled an expedition to the eastern Cascades, there were wildfires burning out of control. This has happened every summer since 2012. My sympathies go out to those who lost loved ones, pets, livestock, and property and thank you so much to the heroic firefighters, emergency personnel, and the communities that supported them.

My back (muscles and spine) decided it didn't like long road trips. I suffered injuries returning home from Walla Walla.[24] Then, over the Memorial Day weekend of 2016, I made the Chopaka Lake and Colville trip (M17). The drive on the way herniated the disk at my L3 vertebrae. This is an injury I'm dealing with currently and may need fusion surgery. In my last steps that Memorial Day Weekend, I hobbled my way up to the statue on Disautel Pass and ended up crawling back into my car due to pain and immobility.

In June of 2016, I suffered a diverticulitis attack that put me in the emergency room. Up until that point in my life I had celebrated the fact that I'd never spent a single night in a hospital. The diverticulum was perforated which led to an abscess in my abdominal cavity. This hospitalized me for four days and the entire time I was there, my surgeon reminded me that I had a 50/50 chance of needing surgery. I escaped that malady uncut. The worst part was it directly affected a

---

[24] I logged over just under 1000 miles on that trip!

Mount Saint Helens expedition that was on the calendar. The first International Bigfoot Conference had been scheduled in Kennewick. Adam was the keynote speaker and I whole-heartedly intended on attending. Adam and I hatched a plan for him to fly into Seattle a few days before the conference. We would then take a couple of days to drive there via Mount Saint Helens where we planned to visit Ape Canyon and do some high altitude summer hiking in a legitimate Bigfoot investigation.

    I missed an entire month of work in June and was fearful that I wasn't healthy enough to camp and hike. In all honesty, had I suffered that diverticulitis attack on some sort of remote backpack trip, I could have died. I couldn't have walked out on my own, I know that. I didn't want to put Adam in that sort of position, especially concerning it could affect his arrival time at the conference. Begrudgingly, I canceled out the ultimate Bigfoot road trip plans. It is unfortunate. That trip would have been the book's final chapter.

    My grandmother, Marge, whom I wrote about, died on September 4th, 2015. She was very interested in seeing this book reach fruition. She was proud of me and definitely believed in the possibility of Sasquatch. "I definitely think it's a possibility," she told me, "who knows what all is out there?" Her mind was sharp when she went and, at age 91, she died in her sleep. She was born in 1924. This was the same year as the attack on Ape Canyon. A bit of personal serendipity only relevant to myself but, superstitious as it may seem, I still pay attention to strange coincidences.

Aside from the herniated disc, I'm healthy now. In August of 2017, I finally made it to the south side of Mount Saint Helens without any health calamities or forest fires. There were no hunters to contend with. I hiked the Ape Canyon Trail and put in 351 floors and 15 and a half miles that day. [25]

***

Before we delve too deeply into my south side exploits, let's talk about my stance on the north side. Undoubtedly, the entirety of the woods surrounding Mount Saint Helens has a historical presence and many entries into the journals of wildman lore.

Green refers to a journal entry by Paul Kane in 1847. Kane states he tried to hire an Indian (his word, not mine) guide to get him closer to Mount Saint Helens. He found difficulty when the natives vehemently refused due to what the author referred to as "superstitions."

"These superstitions are taken from the statement of a man who, they say, went to the mountain with another and escaped the fate of his companion who was eaten by the 'Skoocooms or evil genii" Kane writes: "I offered a considerable bribe to any Indian who would accompany me in its exploration, but could not find one hardy enough to venture" (Green, The Sasquatch File, p. 5).

Many of the north side sightings, historically, stemmed from the shores of Spirit Lake. Many of the witnesses were involved in the YMCA camp (Camp Loowit), which, in my opinion, was the most picturesque and iconic summer camp that ever existed. Ground-breaking occurred in 1929. I'd be remiss if I didn't mention Harry Truman's Lodge. Truman, a World War I veteran, had never been the president but he loved his lodge, his cats, and his antique player piano. And visitors loved Harry. Then his beloved mountain shook and coughed to life. Harry refused to leave his lodge. During evacuations, this story was understandable human-interest fodder for all the local news outlets[26].

Camp Loowit celebrated a 50-year reunion in 1979 and, in a seemingly cruel irony, had started a massive renovation facilitating upgrades and replacing aging

---

[25] Thanks Fitbit!

[26] If still available, check out the YouTube video: *Harry R. Truman and His Spirit Lake Lodge*.

cabins (Borgaard, 2010). On May 18th, 1980 a pyroclastic flow of pulverized rock, trees, and poisonous, super-heated gasses raced ahead of an apocalyptic landslide. Seconds late, the entire summit of Mount Saint Helens slammed into the lake. This was how the camp, the lodge, and Mr. Truman met their end. On that day 57 people died which I report to you with solemn respect.

***

In the mid-1950s, Paul McGuire reported to John Greene that he had seen a white Sasquatch between Coldwater Lookout and Saint Helen's Lake. He initially thought he was seeing an albino bear. In 1963 a report in the Oregon Journal reported a group of Boy Scouts having been frightened by an "ape-man" (Green, The Sasquatch File, 1973).

There are dozens of reports I could share about Mount Saint Helens' north side. But it isn't there anymore. One awful but awesome May afternoon transformed the region into something new. True, the flora and fauna have recovered and together they've helped to stabilize the geology and hydrology within the blast zone. Is it still a Sasquatch haven?

It's the sheer bulk of tourism and visitation concentrated on the north side that I think limits any substantial Bigfoot presence.

On average, 750,000 visitors view the volcano and its surrounding landscape each year within the monument and surrounding forest service facilities.[27] From this number, some 220,000 to 230,000 monument passes are purchased to drive WA 504 inside the monument. I spoke with Kristine Cochrane. She manages public records and staffs the Coldwater Science and Learning Center and she reported these numbers to me. These numbers are low to be sure. We spoke about troublesome car counters (the ones I'm familiar which counted cars, not people[28]), and the fact that this data comes from purchased passes. Children are not required to have a pass to enter the monument, only each adult. Furthermore, certain annual passes allow unlimited access for the owner of the vehicle who displays said pass. Taking into consideration school field trips, literally busloads of children, there are many heads uncounted.

---

[27] Simple Google search.
[28] Washington State Parks had an algorithm to extrapolate the number of park visitors from these primitive car counters. I believe, but could be mistaken, that the average was to be 3.5 people per vehicle. This is heavily flawed because the numbers from the counter recorded trailers, vehicles with more than 2 axles, employees and park vehicles, and vehicles headed the other direction which crossed the center. Often times the units simply failed. The process, I feel is about as useful as trying to predict the number of socks in a household by weighing lint.

So, out of the roughly 750,000 visitor-estimate, more than half of the tourists find themselves viewing the crater and traveling one road, WA 504, toward any number of awe-inspiring and educational opportunities, likely on their way to the last stop, the Johnston Ridge Observatory. Not surprisingly, most visitation occurs between late May and September.

My point is, hundreds of thousands of eyes are trained on the landscape of WA 504 and Saint Helens' yawning north face as the trip is slowly traversed from stop to stop.

Consider this: Nationally, Bigfoot reports spike in the summer. Are there more Bigfoot in the summer? Doubtful. There are more people to see or sometimes think they saw Sasquatch. This is conjecture on my part but it's reasonable to assume that these creatures attempt to avoid the crowds. Summer visitors don't seem to spike the sighting reports here. I can't speak for how devastatingly the eruption affected the Sasquatch population but I do earnestly feel that, when the ash settled, the ensuing turnstile human presence pushed them outward to more inaccessible areas.

Visit Mount Saint Helens. Do it. Visit the blast zone. Make the drive to the observatory. I implore you. It's well worth the price of admission[29]. I even encourage you to seek the Sasquatch. I'd love it if you proved me wrong.

***

---

[29] $8 per adult, per day, as of fall, 2017.

Figure 25: Parked atop the Lahar Plane.

Let's revisit the southern side. Undeniably the eruption impacted all of the volcano and Ape Canyon, as it existed before, was erased by the blast which traveled over hillsides, valley to valley. Lahars further scoured the landscape which is still evident today. The Ape Canyon hike takes you along the lahar-scarred plain and every gouge in the mountain is a reminder of how much snow, rocks, and vegetation were begrudgingly washed away in super-heated mud.

The south side is heavily used, don't get me wrong. Some of the country's most scenic trails exist here and climbers flock to the bivouac for an early morning climb to the summit of the volcano. Most tourists visit the world's largest lava tube, Ape Cave. Here, though, it's easier to spread out and explore forest service roads. Mid-week during the non-peak season, you can easily find yourself on a trail all alone.

WA 503 and NF 90 are your main arteries for south side access. While I believe searching the volcano's gravelly paths to the north of these roads is worthwhile, searching to the south is out of this world.

Wired for Weird

If a place has one kind of weird, it usually has others.

On a ranch, less than six miles from Rock Lake (two miles as the magpie flies), there were barns and a farmhouse and behind that farmhouse, a pond stocked with trout. Beyond that pond were wheat and barley fields that ran for hundreds of miles like Mother Nature's patchwork quilt. My grandma prepared for bed. Grandad, Pete, was already snoring away. It was late summer and this meant harvest. The farmers worked as long of days as they could to beat the rain, get the crop put away and keep the costs down so as to turn a profit on their grain sales. It was not unusual for a combine operator to stay out after dusk. For this reason, the machine is covered in lights. There are lights on the cab and header ranging from white to amber and there are red lights on the rear of the machine. Seeing a fleet of combines at night is somewhat otherworldly. This is what my grandmother first thought she saw through the plate glass window in the bedroom. Lights came over the hill and her first instinct was the perfectly reasonable assumption that it was a combine coming in for the night.

Combines are loud. They use powerful diesel engines and an array of belts, pulleys, and hydraulics. A combine is about as silent as a mosquito is likable. She didn't, however, hear the diesel engine, the belts, the pulleys, the gears, and the hydraulics or the huge rubber tires crushing the stubble. She became gravely transfixed. What she was seeing but not hearing was a *craft*. Not any piece of farm equipment which should exist on this earth, rather a well-lit and very silent "something" floated toward that large window. "Pete! Pete! Wake up and look at this!" My grandma elbowed him. Grandad snorted into reluctant consciousness.

"Well I'll be dammed" he responded in a less-than-astonished-manner and then went back to sleep. Now the craft was gone. If I may translate my grandad's blasé, *I'll be damned* response: they DO exist. What they saw was a UFO in the sense that is was an <u>object</u> that <u>flew</u> and was, to them, <u>unidentifiable</u>. I did not witness the event but their interpretation that it could have been an extraterrestrial conveyance, given the circumstances, is forgivable and perhaps even possible. My mother, having heard grandma's story on numerous occasions, was able to clarify for me what this craft looked like. She described, and even drew, a chevron-like wing with lights on the bottom, middle and top. I know what you're thinking: STEALTH BOMBER! Or at least some other secretive wing-shaped aircraft belonging to the air force, either ours or theirs. The length of the object was vertical, meaning the *aircraft* would have been on its side. It was also very low to the ground and slow. Any conventional aircraft, flown under the physics which contemporary airplanes are still mired to, would have lost lift and dug its wingtip into the loam. A brilliant explosion, a football field worth of wreckage and certainly an ensuing investigation would have occurred. Red, green and white lights should've been present on a human aircraft. Green on the right and red on the left are a navigational arrangement that tells an observer which direction the vehicle is traveling. Maritime vessels (boats) utilize the same system (on bow and stern). My grandfather, having spent a great deal of time working on the air force base was well accustomed to the sight of SAC bombers landing and taking off. As was my grandmother. B-52's routinely roared overhead in and out of Fairchild, keeping a 24-hour nuclear presence in the skies.

My grandad's sudden realization that humanity was not alone in the universe was so matter-of-fact because his belief system had so readily allowed for it. This is an admirable state of mind given the time period.

My grandma once told me a story. "Your grandad and I use to go park out in the fields and *neck*[30]. We'd look up at the moon. One time he said...ya' know, we're going to put a man up there someday.' He took all of the romance out of the moon."

***

In the early '90s my friend Bill and I camped at Rock Lake in what was charmingly named "Slaughterhouse Bay." The land belonged to a local farm family who had been friends with my family since our ancestors homesteaded the area. Their land, which they used to pasture their cattle, led down to a peaceful gully. Its basalt bluffs provided a sheltered bay, a safe harbor, from the lake's notorious squalls. The land is vehemently posted to all hunting and trespassers

---

[30] Kissing, "making out."

but my family, in appreciation of decades of cooperation, loyalty, and friendship, were allowed to use the private respite. Now, I've painted a picture of this secret fishing hole as some sort of oasis or Shangri-La but it's truly the case of beauty being within the eye of the beholder since, on any given occasion, we'd have to deal with rattlesnakes, ticks, packrats, cow patties, and marauding cattle expecting an alfalfa handout. Also, as is my driving theme here, it had once actually held a slaughterhouse. The unappealing name was enough to keep away under-motivated trespassers. Beyond that, making one's trek more treacherous were the barbed wire fence, the locked gate and the fact that the "road" was only a road inasmuch as it was the path in which the farmer had decided he was the least likely to get stuck. It was rough and presented obstacles like basalt boulders and muddy, cow manure-filled wallers.

Back to Bill and me. By "camped" I mean that we were going to sleep in the back of my father's Dodge truck under the canopy. We had a tarp attached like a rainfly and we had our fishing lines in the water. We were older teenagers at the time but I was respectful enough to the privilege I was granted not to turn this into a beer-fueled rampage. It was just the two of us this night and we lacked any *real adult* supervision. I'd like to tell you that we'd dined on freshly-caught trout butter-fried in a cast iron pan over the campfire like the boys you'd read about in a Kjeglaard novel[31] but alas, we probably feasted on Hot Wheels Cereal ™ that my dad purchased at the air force base for 89 cents a box.

We each told campfire stories and darkness fell, which was coincidentally about the time the wind and clouds rolled in. We retreated to the *safety* of the pickup truck and laid in our sleeping bags continuing our conversation. The best story I'd been saving for last and I told Bill about a terrifying, and very true, encounter my uncle had had while camped at the head of this very lake. I really emphasized the truthfulness of his account for he really was *a religious man not prone to lying*.

More on his story in a bit.

Well, the story did our nerves no good and we got the creeps, a theme that will pop up a few more times in this book. It didn't help matters that the storm rolled in and the gusting, horrible wind made demonic howls and clawed at our tarp, much like the Blair Witch who wouldn't enter into our pop-culture

---

[31] Jim Kjeglarrd (1910 to 1959) was a prolific author of young adult literature. He wrote boy-and-dog adventure stories that very much had a frontier feel to them. These stories appealed to lads like myself and were frequently checked out of my elementary school's library. While my sister was reading *Ralph S. Mouse* books (Beverly Cleary) I was reading Kjeglarrd's *Snow Dog* and *Big Red*.

consciousness for another couple of decades. Both of us were equally freaked out. The wind made the tarp flutter, snap and shake in such a seemingly angry way we were certain we'd somehow upset the spirits of the natives who used this bay long before us. "Bill, what the hell IS that!" I stammered as the howls and possession of the tarp worsened. Lightning strikes illuminated the basalt cliffs and the thunder roared like cannon fire through the canyon.

It was just the two of us, and it need not be spoken, but as long as neither of us blabbed about it to our friends, we could retreat to a safer location without suffering too much mockery. There was a public landing to the southwest of the bay at the "foot" of the lake. It was outside the locked gate, past the barbed wire fence, over the boulders and mucky cow-manure wallers. We'd have to drive the inhospitable wagon trail at night, IN A SPRING THUNDERSTORM, mind you, but we could potentially retreat to a safer location.

My father had mentioned, before Bill and I embarked on this adventure, that my uncle and aunt were camped in a Scamper[32] at the landing. So, this was to where Bill and I retreated. We did so at an entirely unsafe speed stripping years of usefulness away from my father's truck as well as anything superfluous that may have been hanging below the truck's underbelly. Any cables, wires or lesser-reinforced pieces of sheet metal were now part of the formidable landscape.

We rolled into the gravel parking area at the public landing about as quietly as a firetruck arriving at a burning fireworks factory. Having parked next to the only trailer I could surmise was a bona fide *Scamper*, Bill and I spilled out of the cab of the truck, shook off the heebie-jeebies and headed toward the truck's bed to revisit the idea of a good night's sleep. It was very dark, but a wide-shouldered, masculine silhouette was stirring outside the scamper tending to ropes and tarps the storm may have damaged on its warpath through the lake valley. He looked at me and, in a pants-peeingly scary voice said "What the flugelhorn are you looking at?!" Now, to be honest, my uncle didn't say "flugelhorn." I'm cleaning it up so that kids might still be able to read this book. The bluest profanity I'd ever heard my uncle exclaim from beneath his Flandersesque mustache was "good gosh almighty!" I was quite taken aback by his aggressive posturing. "Ken, it's me."

"What the flugelhorn do you want?"

"Ken, it's me, Jason…your nephew."

---

[32] The Scamp Company produced lightweight travel trailers. They were small and perfect for a married couple without a copious number of kids. I'm sure my dad is the only one who called it a *Scamper*. It's a little funny, I suppose. I should exploit that.

Secretly Seeking Sasquatch

Finally, in what seemed at least as long and uncomfortable as a traffic stop, my uncle recognized my quivering voice and gave me a solid handshake and warm smile. I introduced my camping companion and explained the circumstances of our unannounced and sudden arrival. He made some reference to the suddenness and nastiness of the storm and excused himself for a moment to go inside the scamper. My aunt was inside and I couldn't quite make out the soft and muffled conversation. I secretly hoped that they were going to invite Bill and me in for a cup of hot chocolate.

My uncle soon reemerged and, much to our mutual pleasure, invited us in for a cup of hot chocolate. One can imagine that the Scamp brand camper is not spacious. But it is efficient. I don't remember the four of us being cramped (scramped?). My aunt greeted us and we sat, her and my uncle on their bed and Bill and me on the dining bench. Ken apologized for his behavior earlier. He explained that he had done a lot of desert camping in California, much of it in the '60s and '70s. He told us that there were a lot of crazies out there and the last thing you wanted was to encounter was one in the dead of the night while camping in the middle of nowhere. His "I'm crazier than you" demonstration was a tool he had used to stave off more than one potential Charles Manson. It was necessary, he explained, to take control of the situation right away. It could always be deescalated later. I had received the full blast of one such preemptive strike.

We sipped our hot chocolate. It's amazing how much a warm drink, electric lights, and generous companions can soothe frayed nerves. We told the story which led up to our hasty retreat. Ken mentioned that there had been more than a few times he had camped on the lake and been spooked by either the weather or some odd occurrence. This was just the opportunity I had been waiting for and I got him to tell the terrifying encounter (the one I eluded to earlier).

This would be a real treat. I had only ever heard this story retold by my mother. She told it with such seriousness and emphasized that Ken, while loving a good prank now and then, wouldn't lie in such a way or fabricate anything like this. She understood him in only the way a sister could understand a brother and knew he was telling the truth.

My uncle leaned forward with his elbows on his knees and, with what seemed like a slightly uncomfortable confession, told his tale.

In the 1960's he and his not-long-out-of high school friends took advantage of Ken's naval leave for some guy time. He and some buddies had decided to hike along the railroad tracks which skirted the murky green depths to a cabin located at the head of the lake. I always imagined the movie *Stand by Me* when trying to picture the scene. It was about a 9-mile walk and I know it had knee-shaking heights that I doubt I could stomach. The cabin had long since been abandoned and for all I know, it had belonged to a fur trader a century ago because, by any modern conveyance other than boat or dirt bike, it was inaccessible.

The boys reached the cabin before nightfall and did some fishing and swimming. By the time darkness crept over the bluffs, they bedded down inside the dusty chantey. Sleep consumed all but one and my uncle lay awake listening to the symphony of nighttime noises. Frogs croaked incessantly and crickets played back up. Even the horned owl chimed in occasionally. But in unison, the wilderness fell deathly quiet. The silence, when experienced like this, is startling. My uncle listened intently from his sleeping bag, the snores and breaths of his companions and his own beating heart were the only noises he could make out now.

My uncle now, in telling the story, grew gravely serious. He reported it matter-of-factly with zero hyperbole. Just like me telling you the "green glowing *something* story." He said there was a brilliant red light from outside. It bathed the cabin in red light. Red light spilled between the logs and missing chinking of the cabin walls. His friends did not stir. He was terrified. There was no sound. The next thing he knew, it was daylight. Hours had seemingly passed in an instant.

***

This is important. My uncle simply hadn't heard of alien abduction or the concept of missing time at this point in his life. As I said, it happened in the mid-1960s. And I know what you're thinking! It wasn't some acid trip. Let me reiterate. My uncle was athletic, honest and a straight-arrow. He served our country dutifully in the U.S. Navy, was privy to military secrets and developed a love of the bible and spirituality. I'm hesitant to guess what exactly my uncle experienced but it wasn't a drug-induced hallucination and he wasn't lying to me. Much like historical Sasquatch accounts, there weren't any famous cases preceding this incident, at least none that were available for my uncle to have been subconsciously influenced by. I'm fully aware of the place I've led you to and the one I'm dancing around but for lack of a better descriptor at this point let's call it an alien (or UFO) abduction. The most famous of these cases is the Betty and Barney Hill incident. Whatever happened to the Hills in 1961, the story didn't surface for several years. In 1964 the couple actually underwent therapy for the haunting dreams and emotional trauma which followed their encounter. It was during hypnotic sessions that the couple (separately) relayed very similar and equally horrifying stories that thrust the terms "alien abduction" and "missing time" into our cultural vernacular.

Other stories emerged in the 1970s. Travis Walton's *Fire in the Sky* (1975) incident certainly isn't dissimilar and the Allagash Waterway Abduction (1976) practically reads like a transcript penned from my uncle's account.

My mother developed an interest in subjects like this and read of these accounts in her adult life. Knowing how hypnosis was being used to treat trauma and recover memories of these events, she encouraged my uncle to undergo such a session.

***

My uncle, sitting next to his wife, leaning in with his elbows on his knees, his hands clasped together, as if in prayer, looked gravely at Bill and me and said "You know, Linda (my mom) tried to convince me to undergo hypnosis so I might remember what happened in that missing time…I'm not sure I want to remember."

To date and to my best knowledge my uncle hasn't revisited the matter and I know he doesn't talk of this often, at least outside of his home.

I know these aren't Bigfoot stories but I wanted you to understand a little more about me and where I come from. I wanted you to understand how a little bit of weird has followed me around so, it's no surprise that I'd eventually become a Bigfoot researcher and pen a book on the subject. I know I promised that I wouldn't tie Sasquatch to the UFO phenomenon and I don't believe I have. I did tell you UFO stories though and here's my point: some places are just wired for weird. If a place has one type of weird it usually has others. Maybe Bigfoot inhabits the scabby pine forests near Rock Lake. Maybe I should look.

Jason M. Burke

The Ballad of Cripplefoot

The Bossburg footprints present a case of unilateral skewfoot that may have arisen from a crushing injury or perhaps a spinal cord lesion resulting in distal neuropathy.

-Dr. Jeff Meldrum

In the snowy November of 1969, something was definitely stomping, or limping rather, around the little town Bossburg (M18) just shy of 100 miles north of Spokane. The story goes that a local Butcher stumbled upon some peculiar Bigfoot prints near the community's garbage dump. One can hardly blame those early witnesses for jumping to this obvious conclusion: that there was a badly crippled Bigfoot who was mooching food scraps from the dump.

While the nickname lacks modern-day sensitivity, Cripplefoot became a sort of unofficial mascot accompanying a mini Bigfoot frenzy in northeastern Washington in 1969. And, as with most Sasquatch firestorms, there is no shortage of polarized opinions, alleged frauds, and comical interactions so as to contaminate the whole episode.

The founding fathers of Bigfoot research descended on the town. Rene' Dahinden, Grover Krantz, Peter Byrne, Roger Patterson, and Dr. John Napier all had parts to play like unwilling actors in an improvised farce. The entirety of the circus that developed is so convoluted and time-consuming that I'm not going to even attempt to retell the whole tale here. Please consult my bibliography for further readings. In extreme brevity, a man named Ivan Marx came onto the scene boasting claims of having a living Bigfoot trapped and incapacitated and began auctioning access to the hidden beast to the highest bidder. This split the researchers into two competing camps. Marx's claims evolved into assertions of a frozen Sasquatch foot he could produce (presumably from the aforementioned *incapacitated* creature) and films showcasing groundbreaking footage. According to Napier's account (Napier, Startling Evidence of Another Form of Life on Earth Now: Bigfoot, p. 94) rivalries formed, friendships disintegrated and the town of Bossburg just got plain sick of the whole deal. In the end, Marx never produced a specimen and his films are largely considered in the Bigfoot field to be mediocre fakes.

So, was the whole thing a hoax? Let's toss out everything except for the casts taken from the Cripplefoot prints. I've seen casts of these prints and they are remarkable. There's an oft-used quote from Napier stating "It is very difficult to conceive of a hoaxer so subtle, so knowledgeable and so sick who would deliberately fake a footprint of this nature. I suppose it is possible but it is so unlikely that I am prepared to discount it."

I asked Dr. Meldrum about the Bossburg incident and Cripplefoot. "The Bossburg footprints present a case of unilateral skewfoot that may have arisen from a crushing injury or perhaps a spinal cord lesion resulting in distal neuropathy. I have discussed this case at length with podiatrists and orthopedic surgeons. Not only is the pathology compelling, but the distinctions in proportion -- i.e., breadth of heel, relative length of toes and hind foot -- lack of a longitudinal arch, are consistent with a model of the Sasquatch foot inferred from numerous independent cases."

The footprints still stand as the greatest piece of evidence suggesting, at least some of the incredible story is true. Many people maintain that at the core of any lie is at least a kernel of truth. It's unfortunate, though not uncommon, in the Sasquatch conundrum that, what seems to be a bona fide event or series of events occur that inspire a spree of hoaxes, hysteria, and outlandish claims that discredits the entire affair.

I'll let you be the judge as to what really occurred in northeastern Washington all those decades ago. Fortunately, there are other Bigfoot sightings and accounts to support the notion that these creatures have really been, and may still be there.

There are reports separate from the Bossburg incident.

Admittedly, I do believe activity on the Bossburg side of Lake Roosevelt (The Columbia River) has cooled substantially since the '60s. There is, however, a great value in following WA-20 west out of Kettle Falls and heading over Sherman Pass (M18). A winter road crossing was recorded in 1971 and in 1972, Famed Yeti Tracker, Peter Byrne wrote of a sighting on Sherman Pass in *Explorers Journal* (Bord, pp. 264-265).

Personally, long ago, I had an experience on Sherman Creek camped just off of Sherman Pass. It was the summer before my senior year. *Thunderstruck* was on the radio so, in route to the campsite I bought AC-DC's *The Razors Edge* cassette at a drug store and blasted it through the Audiovox speakers in my Plymouth Champ.

I was with my not-then-brother-in-law-who-is-now-my-bother-in-law-of-23-years: Phil. Phil and I found a remote campsite on Sherman Creek. It was in the Colville National Forest so you were able to just claim a site. No fee. No paperwork[33]. The little creek had little trout. It was perfect and we seemed to be alone. We saw no other campers, very little traffic, and not a single park ranger.

It was on the morning after the first night that Phil informed me of a somewhat spooky occurrence. Late into the night or early in the morning hours he had heard someone or *something* walk through our campsite. He said it definitely walked on two feet. For a moment he saw a silhouette against the tent's nylon wall. I recall him describing the figure as tall but I don't recall any description of a hulking physique. It paused, scuffled and then walked in the direction of the deep dark woods. Definitely not the road.

We weren't quick to blame Bigfoot, however, these words were spoken by both of us and have been spoken many times since: "I'm not saying it was Bigfoot but it would have been creepier if it was a person." This still rings true. There weren't other sites to access. A ranger might have logged our presence in whatever unnamed site we were in but he or she wouldn't have had any reasonable suspicion to enter our site at that hour. Why would they then walk into the woods?! An uninvited person with no authority walking into our site, presumably without a vehicle, is scary and sounds dangerous. Perhaps a hitchhiking vagrant was foraging for beer and lunchmeat but this, to me, is disturbing as we were so vulnerable while we slept. It's not a Bigfoot story but it is a personal experience. If the creature: Sasquatch was documented by zoology tomorrow, I'd feel confident telling you one had visited that dark night decades ago.

Explore Sherman Pass.

---

[33] You had better check on this. That was almost 30 years ago.

The Land of Okanogan

Not necessarily *close* and not necessarily *far* from Kettle Falls proper is the Canadian Border and a little lake called "Chopaka." On Memorial Day (May 26) of 1996, the Pate family; Lori and Owen, videotaped what they consider to be a Sasquatch sprinting across a steep hillside which borders the mountain lake.

Close examination, most of which was conducted by Jeff Meldrum and contributors to *Legend Meets Science (2001 televised documentary)* state a case that the subject who runs across a treeless gap on the hillside, is a female Sasquatch who transfers a Sasquatch child from her hip to her shoulders.

While the video alone, could have fallen into obscurity due to ambiguity, there is eyewitness testimony to strengthen the case. Tom Lines, a witness present that day, observed the figure through binoculars and adamantly describes a Bigfoot rather than a human in a sweatshirt or other type of hoaxy garb.

This is certainly a case of straining at the pixels because VHS wasn't the clearest recording medium in amateur hands and, if you're anything like my family, the "tape" loaded in the camera already has something like *Star Trek: The Next Generation* recorded on to it. So, starting with a recording limited by quality, technology and the great distance of the subject, there are essentially two possibilities to the events the Pate family recorded: either it was a sprinting Sasquatch who transfers something, presumably a child or infant onto his or her shoulders or it was a human who, pulled off the stunt, on which is essentially mountain goat territory, and shifted either a backpack or flipped back a costume mask all without tripping and breaking their leg, mid-shin, in a gopher hole.

The reason any conjecture exists as to *what*, exactly, the subject *does* just before reaching the far tree line is important because careful examination suggests the subject filmed is a diminutive 5'3" and grows by 8" at the end of the run. Being 5'3" doesn't rule out a Bigfoot any more than it *does* a person. The event is covered meticulously by Dr. Meldrum in his book and a great deal more in the earlier documentary. I highly recommend you check out both.

All of this occurs east of the Cascade Mountains. If you've crossed the Cascades, you're well aware of how quickly the climate and geology change as you crest the summit and descend into central Washington. Clouds dump their rain on the coast and their snow on the mountains, what blows into places like Ellensburg, Wenatchee and Yakima is dry air. Central Washington, more accurately referred to as the Columbia Basin, constitutes a desert. It is hot in the summer and cold in the winter. It is both sparse in rainfall, annually, and can receive heavy snowfall in the winter. If it weren't for the rivers, which provide ample irrigation for bumper crops of apples, potatoes, hops, wine grapes, and onions, it's hard to see what resources humans could eek from the land.

The summers are the hottest at the lowest elevations within the basin. Here, the desert conditions are the most evident and extreme. The higher you climb out of the valleys the more trees you'll encounter, most of which are pine. According to the Washington State Department of Natural Resources, the Ponderosa Pine is the most populous and among the heartiest trees in the state. It has remarkable drought resistance and can grow on the rockiest and most formidable rock outcroppings.

Ponderosas succeed because of their knack for enduring the harsh extremes of central Washington desert life. When you walk in a pine forest east of the Cascades, typically, the groundcover is sparse and needles from the pines litter the forest floor. So, the pine forests in eastern Washington (as the all-encompassing term) are arid and suffer temperature extremes from (uncommon but not unheard of) 105 degrees Fahrenheit into the double integer negatives. To be fair, Western Washington can face the same extremes but these margins are considerably rarer and the number of days spent at either extreme is fewer. Because of this, Western Washington's weather is considered mild.

Bigfoot is said to share the same habitat and elevations as North America's black bear. By and large, Sasquatch sightings (and encounters) fall into bear country. One could extrapolate that they have a similar diet. I'd be remiss, as well, if I didn't mention that bears could also be blamed for a portion, possibly a large number, of Bigfoot sightings. Obviously, bears are at home in this environment. Bears, however, hibernate in the winter. But does the Sasquatch hibernate?

Meldrum, as of 2006, seemed very open to the idea of Sasquatch hibernation. Citing the diversity of mammals who hibernate and that humans share many of the genes that allow mammals to enter a state of hibernation known as "topor." Unlocking the secrets to human hibernation may be imperative if the human race is to explore deep space. Meldrum concludes "hibernation in a large primate inhabiting the northern latitudes may not be so far-fetched a proposition (Meldrum, p. 3238)."

In 2006, all within 35 miles of Omak (M18), there were a total of six experiences reported to the BFRO from June to October. Only half were actual sightings and the other half consisted of unexplained encounters. Six isn't a lot, but these events occurred over a couple of months. That seems like a spree. I feel these sprees most often indicate Sasquatch passing through.

In the arid pine forests, especially those bordering the Columbia Basin, Sasquatch may be much more transient, rare but not unheard of. While they're adept at surviving winter and the relative harshness of their environment, I believe it is reasonable to assume they seek respite from brutal heat and heavy snow. Just following the well-established cycle of elk migration suggests it would behoove a large mammal to seek higher elevation in the summer and lower elevations in the winter. In central Washington though, there is relatively little tree cover at the lower elevations. In the harshest of winters, low elevation pine forests may offer very little by way of reprieve. So, why not hike into more favorable areas like the western slopes of the Cascades? The bears, they all go to sleep.

This is the long way of saying that I believe that Sasquatch numbers are fewer in areas with extreme climates and that sightings, in Washington's arid forests, occur when Bigfoot happens to pass through and, in the case of clustered occurrences, take up temporary residence where resources are favorable. Any further explanation as to *why* could include food, water, desire to find companionship, and birthing would rank highly on the list of reasonable possibilities.

So, in a geographical region I assign to the Okanogan, the question remains: are there any Sasquatch there? My answer is yes. You just have to know where to look. Chopaka Lake (M17) has produced what I would call a silver standard video. While limited by its technology, and no less controversial, the Patterson/Gimlin footage from those two cowboys in Northern California, is, of course, the gold standard. We're not even going to pay homage to the bronze in this publication. You're welcome to dig around on YouTube.

***

In addition to the Pate's video, a notable sighting occurred a week before by a fisherman on the same lake (BFRO #16994). From there, the sightings are scattered in various directions out of Omak, in the mountains, and near the creeks and lakes.

Okanagan, as it is spelled when referring to its indigenous members, is the name for the larger portion of the tribe which includes Native Americans of the

Confederated Tribes of the Colville and their First Nation Canadian cousins. Collectively, they're known as the Okanagans.

Anyone who has read enough about the subject of Sasquatch has come across references to *The Spokane Indians: Children of the Sun*, co-authored by A.J. Youngson Brown and Robert H, Rudy, wherein the publication quotes a letter penned by Reverend Elkwanah Walker who was stationed at Fort Colville as a missionary to the Spokan people. Walker explains about a superstition of the natives who tell him about "a race of giants" portrayed as "men stealers" who have a taste for raw salmon which they steal from the nets. The visitors announce their presence with three whistles and often throw stones at the tribal houses. The Spokans, according to Walker said that these giants come from "a certain mountain to the west of us" (Meldrum, p. 1328).

While a "certain mountain west of us" is an ambiguous description, to say the least, *mountains to the west* would include the Kettle River Range (which Sherman Pass crosses), Okanogan Range (Disautel Pass), the Monashee Mountains (Chopaka Lake), and the Cascades.

Figure 26: You're hereby challenged to find this statue!

Impression Pun

"The owls are not what they seem."

-Twin Peaks, a message for Agent Copper from the ether.

Whether you believe in Bigfoot or not, you'd be a bovine, clodpated, citified moron[34] if you didn't at least bring a camera on your Bigfoot road trip. In its earliest stages, there was no memoir intended in this book. Nor was there a presumption that the reader would evolve beyond a curious motorist into a budding researcher and citizen scientist. I didn't intend on becoming a researcher either. It just happened. I enjoy doing this. Through the process, old stories leaped into my consciousness and the memoir portions of this book took shape. As a researcher, I made so very many mistakes and learned so much. So, the *beginner's guide* portions gained inclusion.

What I've learned most is *what to bring with you*. Here are some suggestions that will help, should you find yourself looking more and more often for the beast. First, we'll discuss process a bit then I'll include a checklist for your first forays into the Bigfootverse.

Camera:

Seriously, pack a camera. And don't give me a "my cellphone has a 15 megaquad camera with night-vision video." I don't care. You still need a camera. A cellphone camera is simply too slow. My wife has snapped "quick" photos of me with her phone and, by the time she makes it through the screen saver and

---

[34] There's a *Doc Hollywood* reference in there.

clicks the photo, I have aged noticeably in the image that's recorded. Believe me, in the 5 year-debacle that produced this book, I've tried to make my cellphone camera the go-to, right-there-at-the-ready tool of no refute. The camera is good but the widget often drifts off the home screen (I'm inclined to blame my youngest son) or I mistakenly press my similarly-colored email shortcut. Lastly, how many times have you opened your camera only to see your face on the screen and not the subject you wish to photograph? The transition from selfie mode to normal shooting takes immeasurably valuable seconds. Obviously, if this all you have and the creature walks right in front of you, use your cellphone! Take video!

Your cellphone cam is your backup. My preferred method is to keep my digital camera on the video setting and, should Sasquatch ever appear in front of me, I'm not going to stop rolling until the card is out of memory. Ever since the Patterson/Gimlin footage ignited the most controversial Sasquatch firestorm, film (by which I mean video) is going to be scrutinized and criticized no matter how convincing it is. But photo stills will be even worse. At least with the video, you may provide clues like sounds and the animal's locomotion and physical response which will add to your credibility. A photo, to skeptics, is always going to be a man in a monkey suit, a stump, or someone in a "hoody."[35] Even two-dimensional silhouettes have been photographed and passed along as the real deal in some online circles. So, at a bare minimum, carry a high-megapixel digital camera with video setting. It's preferable that the camera has a good telescopic lens. Have it ready, accessible, and know how to use it.

I carry 2 cameras (not counting my smartphone backup)[36]. One I chose for its telescopic qualities and the second I chose for its quick ease-of-use and pocketability. If other people are with you and Bigfoot makes an appearance, roll as many cameras as you can. You still need to be mindful enough to provide a quality observation, so don't glue your eyes to the viewfinder but get good video in addition to your excellent eye-witness account

---

[35] Dear lord, I've used the terms "selfie" and "hoody" in the same chapter. Is the world ending? When did "hooded sweatshirt" or just "sweatshirt" become too time-consuming?! I sound old.

[36] Okay...this is funny. When I wrote that I carried 2 cameras and a phone. Presently, in the field I have a dedicated dash camera in my car and I wear 2 faux-pro cameras (that's what I call these cheaper knock-offs of the famous action camera). This is all in addition to one true camera and a phone. Plus, I have much more confidence with the speed I can reach video recording on my current smartphone. One faux-pro faces forward and one faces behind me on my backpack. These items simply weren't that accessible when I started this journey. This is why I left the original text as it stands and noted my evolution along way.

Recording Sound:

These creatures have long been suspected of making sounds to communicate with others of their species over great distances. Take a listen to the myriad of eerie howls and screams from a Bigfoot research website. In fact, your personal Bigfoot encounter may only be eerie sounds. Sasquatch has been attributed to wood-knocks (a tree limb struck against a tree or other limb), rock-knocks (see also *wood-knocks*), grunts, growls, whoops, and even a guttural language or "ape chatter." Witnesses have reported chimp-like sounds from areas devoid of such primates and researchers say Bigfoot's vocal repertoire can be compared to a macaque or gibbon. In a pinch, turn on your video camera to capture such sounds and your reactions. But the microphone on cameras can be very limited so I recommend having a separate digital voice recorder.

It's helpful that you're familiar with the sounds made by other animals in the forest. Thankfully with internet sources such as YouTube, you don't have to be a fur-tradin' mountain man to learn this familiarity. Some contenders for making eerie sounds who are often misinterpreted for Sasquatch vocalizations are elk, foxes, coyotes, and barred owls. Yes, owls. If you have any experience with these creatures then you're sure to be familiar with at least a portion of their unholy repertoire. They can make some authentically creepy noises and take into account that most of them occur at night. At Saint Edward State Park, I was often kept company by a parliament of barred owls that seemed to show at least a passing curiosity in my park-closing procedures.[37] They were quite ornery in August and would demonstrate this aggression, from time to time, by buzzing hikers at dusk. I hadn't really believed the intensity of reports of close-encounters with the owls until I was "buzzed" by a silent, soft-feathered foe that nearly knocked the ranger hat off of my head. Given my nightly proximity to them, I thought I knew everything I could about these nocturnal raptors. Then one late dark night I was closing the park gate. From deep in the woods I heard an obnoxious "ooh ooh ooh eeh ooh ooh!" It sounded amazingly like the primate enclosures at the zoo. My imagination immediately went to Bigfoot but I quickly dismissed it. This was a large urban park with substantial woods, but we were quite surrounded by miles and miles of cities and suburbs. I mentioned it to my boss/friend, Mohammad the next day. I told him it sounded like a "chimp or a monkey or something!" Now, the neighboring cities of Bellevue and Kirkland are known for being slightly affluent. Bill Gates' Lake Washington home was but a boat ride down the shoreline from us. Couldn't a rich person have released an exotic pet? A monkey

---

[37] A group of owls is called a *parliament*. Look it up!

or ape may freeze over winter, but winters were mild here and this was the end of summer. He dismissed my claims. It wasn't long before Mohammad's wife had her own simian encounter opening the gates before sunrise one early morning. "It sounded just like a monkey!" she said. Mohammad then, given his wife's own testimony, was forced to admit that we both were crazy. But finally, I had an epiphany. While researching this book, I read of certain auditory Sasquatch encounters that were later dismissed by researchers claiming that the culprit was likely a barred owl. I found it odd that suburbanites in Washington could so easily mistake owl calls but it made me curious. I found a website with some recordings and sure enough, the calls known as "caterwauling" are just plain strange. I'm telling you, barred owls can make some freaky noises. Don't be fooled. This doesn't rule out several strange howls and vocalizations recorded over the years; these are still attributed to Bigfoot. I'm just asking that you go into this well-informed and make every effort to rule out the more logical sources first.

Recording Physical Evidence:

Day one of forensics class, I was taught about Locard's exchange principle. Serving as inspiration for Sherlock Holmes, Dr. Edmond Locard advanced criminal investigation techniques substantially by laying down the principle for forensic science: every contact leaves a trace. This applies as much to cryptozoology as it does to criminalistics. If a Bigfoot passes through an area, it will leave a trace. It's up to any researcher or scientist to be observant enough to cue in on these clues.

Earlier I mentioned having found, what I allege to be, a Sasquatch footprint. I had, within my ability, means of casting it and, for reasons difficult to explain, I didn't. Ladies and gentlemen, if you find a print, CAST IT! Or at least contact someone who can. First, though, photograph and document. Fortunately, in this day and digital age, there's really no such thing as wasting film. Remember film? Should you spy something peculiar, snap multiple photos of it. Researchers theorize that Bigfoot often leave behind telltale signs in the way of tree-breaks, limb-breaks, stone piles, and ground nests made from moss and tree boughs. Be careful here. Without a doubt, the VAST majority of tree-breaks, limb-breaks, and rock piles have another explanation other than Sasquatch. All I'm saying is, if something seems odd to you or out of place, there's no harm in photographing it and looking around a bit, a footprint may be around the next corner.

So, you've stumbled upon that big footprint. Or is it a Bigfoot print?!? Step back and look for any other signs. Be careful not to step on any other prints that may be in the area. Most prints aren't going to be of the pretty five-toe museum replica quality. Many times, prints are going to be ambiguous and nearly invisible. It shouldn't be too much of a hassle to carry a tape measure. Measure the print both for width and length (heel to longest toe). Take photos with the tape measure near the print so the scale is immediately evident. Failing that, include something of a predictable size. A pen or dollar bill will work just fine. Your shoe is a poor object to determine scale since, let's say it's a size 10, another size 10 shoe will undoubtedly vary in length. A shoe, however, is better than nothing because you can measure it later. Look for other prints and should you find some, it's time to take more measurements. I'm not going to go into too much detail about *step*, *stride*, *straddle* and *angle of gait*, but it's important to measure from heel to heel of what appears to be the same foot (a left and the next left for example) and the distance from heel to heel of alternating feet (a left to a right or vice versa). This will reveal a great deal to a researcher like the size of the animal, how it moves, and what television programs it has at home on its DVR.

Write down these measurements as well as your observations. Which means you'll need a notebook and pen or your sound recorder or smartphone. Document where you are and the time and date. Also, note the temperature and weather. Take photos in close and back up too including landmarks that will help you and/or a researcher relocate the area later. Other clues may be revealed from your photos that you didn't even notice at the time. Don't forget to look up and all around you. Look for broken limbs or snagged hair. If you feel you're looking at a bona fide Sasquatch print, then try to envision how this thing walked through here. Where it might have placed its hands or did it stop and sit? Scrutinize your surroundings. If you have a GPS device, pin a waypoint or record the coordinates and elevation.

CONTEXT is of extreme importance. If you go around haphazardly collecting hair and fecal samples, you're not going to find anyone willing to test them. There are a lot of hair-covered animals in the forest and every one of them poops. The thing about poop is unless you see the Sasquatch actually in the act of…um, *pooping* then you can't be certain it's from a Bigfoot and, unless it EXTREMELY fresh, the um…*donor's* DNA probably won't be present. What you'll have is a stinky pile of DNA from everything the animal ate. Sure, there could be species-specific parasites within the um…*sample* but who are you going to get to test it? Unless you've seen the animal that produced this scat, it'll be difficult to find somebody to take it off your hands (figuratively) and someone is going to have to float the cost for having it tested. I'm not trying to diminish your excitement over a large turd pile. I'm really not.

I fell victim to poopstaria even after this chapter was written. These next paragraphs are an afterthought. In May of 2017, I was checking out a campsite with Scott. We were scouting the site, which I had booked unseen, for an upcoming Summer investigation where Adam would join us and we'd spend our days looking for evidence and our nights trying to see or hear one of these things and even draw one in. No one was in the campground and Scott and I had free reign to kick around a bit. There was a steep berm directly out the "back" or west side of our site. Atop the berm, I looked down into a swampy area where prickly salmonberry and devil club plants reigned supreme. Next to a cedar was an ASTONISHINGLY large pile of scat. While it was the wrong shape to have come from a horse, it wasn't any smaller in mass than a Clydesdale's evacuation. A substantial animal with a substantial gut made this pile, in one "sitting" and, from the looks of it, very recently. I called Scott and practically tumbled down the hill. I paused and assessed the area, not for danger, mind you, but for hairs or prints or limb-breaks, etc. Scientifically, *bear* scat was on my mind. But I was operating, very excitedly, influenced by the *what-if* possibilities. Certainly, a closer look was warranted. I mean, what if this was Bigfoot poop?! I gloved up and broke out my brand new, bright orange spring blade knife and retrieved a sterile sample cup (liberated from a doctor's office restroom), wiped down the blade with an alcohol wipe and proceeded to poke and prod at sections of the fecal pile. It was fresh, the mucous membrane was there. Whatever it was had just squeezed this out. I felt very confident that it would yield the DNA of its sponsor. I took, what I guessed, would be an adequately-sized sample and started to place it into the cup. That's when I noticed all of the grass. The scat was full of chewed, but not entirely digested, grass. I had a hard time imagining Sasquatch doing this but it was easy to imagine a bear, thoroughly omnivorous, grazing on whatever greens it could stomach. Yes, this was bear scat. Fresh, very fresh bear scat. The reality hit me like a giant clawed-paw to the face. The bear must not be far and one could very much hide, in that thick bramble, not but five feet from my location. Here I was, my back to a very steep, twelve-foot berm with no real evacuation route sans the one I clambered down. Scott helped extricate me and I felt thankful I didn't run afoul of the bear. I don't feel that I have an innate fear of bears. I probably should. My small handful of sightings have occurred from the car. But my carelessness in rushing into that sunken briar could have provoked an ugly confrontation. So, lesson learned.

If you find a footprint (handprint and buttprints too), look carefully for correlating sign. Should you find a strange hair then collect it. It's going to take a

Figure 27: I very nearly ran afoul of this bear in the Northern Cascades. Photo from my trail cam.

body, or a substantial piece of one to scientifically prove Sasquatch's existence but DNA is good enough to get scientists to take notice. Carefully collect hair, feces, fruit with strange bite-marks, etc. into a clean paper bag. Wear gloves and, if using tweezers for sample collection, ensure that they're sterile. I have taken to carrying my multi-tool, I use a Gerber. For one thing, a knife of some sort is of extreme importance. The needle nose pliers are indispensable. I also carry packaged alcohol wipes. So, when a hair is recovered, I wipe down the pliers with the alcohol wipes. I have yet to hear that this process is fallible. Think about *contamination*. You don't want your DNA or any other contaminants to foul the sample. I've heard a very seasoned researcher say "if you touch it with your bare hands, you may as well have licked it." Tape the bag shut and use a marker to write the date, contents, location, etc. Immediately, upon your return home, place these items in the freezer (scat must be dried first).

Jason M. Burke

Casting Prints:

The most important item in your kit, other than a camera, is some sort of casting medium. In the 21st Century, we have more options available than just plaster of Paris or cement. Fortunately, modern casting mediums are lighter. Water, however, still weighs the same. Most commonly, you'll find products named Fix it All, Hydrocal, Hydrostone, Ultracal, Duracal, Quetzacoatl, and Tlahuizcalpantecuhtli. I simply use construction joint compound, a bag of Beadex Silver Set 20 (the *20* means it sets in 20 minutes[38]) that can easily be found in a hardware store. Let's just agree to call it plaster.

So, you've examined your print and have documented it photographically. Always photograph it first. Carefully remove debris if it looks to have blown into or fallen into the print. If it, the twig, tree cone, etc. looks like it has been stepped on, leave it. DO NOT change or enhance the print. Some debris may be revealing, an example would be noting how a pliable foot interacted with a stone. A hoaxer's rigid wooden stamp is unlikely to interact with objects convincingly. Now, forget the notion of walking away with a foot-shaped hunk of plaster. You're actually going to build a circular or oval-shaped frame around the print using plastic strips. These strips can be obtained by cutting up a couple of empty bleach bottles. Really, you can use anything lightweight and flexible to help frame in a mold. The strips should be long and about two to three inches tall. The idea is to paperclip several strips together, forming a wall around the print, which will serve as a form to hold your plaster.

It's helpful at this point to spritz the surface of the print with hairspray. Yes, hairspray. This will help bond the material in which the print was left. This works especially well in sand or dry and dusty soil and will help you produce a cleaner mold. It's still going to have debris stuck all over it, mind you, but the hairspray will help reduce that.

Now, mix the plaster. You're going to need about two parts water to plaster and you're going to have to make some sort of estimate as to *how much* that is. You want to add the powder to the water. Fill your mixing container (bowl, can, plastic bag, etc.) with the water first. Now, with a gloved hand, add the plaster and use your fingers to break up the lumps and mix the powder and water. The trick is not to introduce a lot of air. Bubbles are bad. The ideal consistency should be something like a milkshake or pancake batter. Whichever you prefer. I usually consume both at breakfast. It's best not to get into the trap of adding water then

---

[38] Personal results may vary. Drying time for me (in the field) exceeded one hour.

some powder and then some water and always trying to match the right consistency. I won't hold it against you if you do. I'm reminded of something a defensive tactics instructor once told me, "Just get the cuff on." Let me explain. There's a whole technique to cuffing a violator. It's not particularly complicated but it was practiced a lot in my former agency. An extraordinary level of proficiency was expected at test time as the focus was to keep the officer, violator, and anyone else safe and uninjured. Law enforcement officers are trained, you see, to keep everyone safe. But at the end of the day, if you're fighting a felon, don't fret about technique. Just get the cuffs on. My advice is to you: if you're looking at a bona fide Sasquatch print and there's a snowstorm threatening to erase your evidence, just get the mold poured.

You've taken measurements and photos, placed the plastic ring around the print, and removed troublesome debris and, if available, you've sprayed the print with hairspray, now pour the plaster. If you can't pour it, it's too thick.[39] GENTLY, pour it outside the area of the print and let it spill into the print. Don't pour directly onto any of the print's detail as the weight from the cascading plaster could alter or erase those details. Pour it thick, but not too thick. Too thick and the mold will crumble. Too thin and it will break. Don't sweat it, just do it perfectly the first time.

Infinite factors will affect the dry time of the plaster: heat, humidity, the consistency, thickness of the pour…okay, well mainly just those four. My point is, eventually the plaster will harden. If it feels warm, that's the exothermic reaction to a bunch of chemistry I won't pretend to understand but wait until it's cooled and feels firm enough to handle. Then, wait a little longer. Your situation and environment will dictate how best to lift the mold. You may need a pocket knife to gently pry it from the depression in the ground. Many sources recommended carrying a trowel to aid in prying the mold away from the earth. I scoffed at this at first, thinking it was unnecessary ballast when considering all the other equipment and supplies I was already packing. Then, as I struggled to pry my first cast print from the ground, it became painfully clear how convenient a trowel would be. There are even inexpensive, lightweight plastic ones in the camping aisle at your local sporting goods store. You may be compelled to gently

---

[39] Two things: In my meager opinion, having poured a truly abysmal mold, and if you're to ere, regarding the consistency of your plaster, ere on the side of *too thin*. There's a fine line but thinner mix will record better detail than an overly thick mix. Secondly, you can, in actuality, skip the "mold walls" so long as you have enough plaster to pour up and over the sides of the print, like a big mud puddle. It will take longer to cure but I have been caught, many a time, in the field without those handy little Chlorox bottle strips!

brush off excessive amounts of soil or rock but resist the urge to clean up the mold right now. The underside, the part with the print, is going to be damper than the top and therefore softer. Plus, the plaster is still curing. "Dry" and "hardened" are very different terms than "cured." Excessive handling on your part could erase valuable details of which you may not be aware. Wrap it in newspaper, not plastic, as newspaper will aid in the drying process. Then gently store it away so it travels safely home.

    I once put mine in my toddler's car seat. Don't worry, he wasn't along for this particular adventure. The act, though came back to bite me (metaphorically) because I had inadvertently transported a creepy-crawly back with me who had taken up residence in the area in, on, or around my son's car seat where it lay in wait, biding its time for a taste of my son's flesh. A day or two after my return I had my son in the car and heard his panicked declaration of "*pider, pider*!" Now, for point of clarification, to my son at that time, any bug that flew was a *bee* and any that crawled was a *spider*. Through the rearview mirror I could clearly see the creature, though not a spider, but clearly some larger variety of the forest stink bug species I believe is known as *stinkus stinkus*. The insect wasn't actually on my son but was slowly advancing toward him by way of very deliberate arthropodal steps via the small amount of seat fabric between my son's face and the car's window. Its antennae were testing the air, no doubt honing in on the scent of my son's fear. Bear in mind the boy was harnessed-in and had no way of extricating himself from the situation which, in hindsight, could be the root of his bug phobia that persists to this day. I pulled over reasonably safely, flung open the door (not unlike Superman in the 1978 film[40]) and in an unprecedented moment of daddy-heroism gave the stink bug a satisfying pop between my fingers within a Starbuck's napkin. The rank odor serving as its final protest upon leaving this world.

    Back to the plaster cast…

    In a week or two, you can gently brush off any forest duff. Just don't rinse it off over the dishes in the sink and annoy your partner, parents, or roommates.

    The point is to practice, practice, and practice. The first Sasquatch footprint you encounter shouldn't be the first thing you've ever cast. Lastly, casting a print in the field is much different than practicing under controlled conditions. It would behoove you greatly to practice in the field as well. A deer print will afford you a perfect opportunity and you'll have a nifty souvenir to boot. Furthermore, should you have a scout in the family, this will probably offer an outstanding merit badge opportunity.

---

[40] Superman the Movie, Warner Bros, 1978

This book is meant to be a starting point. It's a way to make your next family road trip thematic and fun. So, at a minimum, you're able to experience Bigfoot culture without getting out of the car. But maybe you want to get out of the car. Maybe you want to be part of the search and attempt to answer some of the questions for yourself.

Here's a list of supplies to assist in your Sasquatch search.

Figure 28: A deer print I cast in the field.

Must-Have:

__Camera: Discussed above, ad nauseam. Have it ready to go in video mode and lots of available memory. You'll be doing yourself a great disservice if you wander into the field with a camera holding every family photo taken since your oldest child's birth.

__An item of known size for scale. You may as well carry a tape measure. A keychain tape would be easy to carry and hard to forget.

__Map(s) GPS will fail you from time to time. Your phone will die. A map will always work so long as you can figure out where you are. A compass is helpful but only if you know how to use it.

__Phone: I advise you so save your phone battery as much as you can. Carry your phone for emergencies, of course, and as an extra camera, and sound recorder, etc.

__Pen and Notebook: Or some way to take notes. Should you find something, take notes!

__An equally open and skeptical mind.

Nice to Have:

__Digital Sound Recorder: I would say you should endeavor to purchase one step above a "voice recorder" which I'd equate to the type you may see on a student's desk during a college lecture. Then, I'd realize how dated that would sound EVEN IF I were describing a wholly digital recorder. I'm sure somewhere at home, I still have a Radio Shack tape recorder that actually takes an answering machine-sized cassette. There are so many words in those preceding sentences that a 20-year-old just won't understand! So, should you take this seriously, go one better than a digital voice recorder and purchase one intended for higher quality replication. I carry a Tascam. These will run you between $100 and $200 but the quality is impressive. A $28 voice recorder will work, to some extent, but won't pick up faint sounds and you will be limited, ultimately by quality and options. I could write nearly a chapter on sound and why it's so important. I'm so very novice but David Ellis, of the Olympic Project, is a true sound expert. I've met and have heard him speak on three occasions. He has even analyzed sound files I have submitted to him. He is an expert. I am not. I will say, after having heard Ellis' collection of suspect sounds, there is something making ape noises on the Olympic Peninsula. And that's all I have to say about that.

__Bait: Be mindful of laws concerning "feeding wildlife" Your Bigfoot bait excuse isn't going to carry very far with the ranger citing you for feeding the wildlife and turning the raccoons into nuisance beggars. There are opportunities here to use your common sense, imagination, or both. You may leave an offering of a peanut butter and jelly sandwich, bacon, or a candy bar. Just understand that infinitely more times than not, the birds and more common mammals are going to mooch what you so considerately or carelessly left behind. Train your camera trap on the bait and try to utilize soft areas of earth that may yield footprints. Also, if there are bears, it is very likely you will get bears. You've been warned.

__Casting medium: a small amount (but enough to do the job) to carry with you. A larger amount in your vehicle or at "base camp." Keep in mind you'll probably need to carry water too. Creeks, when available, are an infinite source of non-potable water that you won't have to carry. Give a Hoot, don't contaminate the water!

___Trowel to pry your cast from the ground.

Figure 29: Setting a camera trap on the Olympic Peninsula. Those boots were not nearly as "waterproof" as they were advertised.

___Trail Cam: In my opinion, this is close to being a necessity. Surely it should be one of your first Bigfoot-specific purchases. Practice with your camera trap at home (in the yard) and understand its settings and how NOT TO wipe out an SD card full of images. Eventually, work up the courage to leave it (legally) in a Bigfooty area for a period of time to see what happens. Fortunately, these items are both smaller and cheaper than they were in the early days of technological Bigfooting.

I'd be remiss if I didn't note that there's a contingent of Bigfooters that believe the creatures can sense, and therefore avoid a camera trap. Certainly, any foreign object you introduce to a creature's habitat (including yourself) is going to emit some sort of scent (and other subtle indicators) that broadcast your presence. A strange, human-associated aroma may be enough to cause a wary ape-man to shy away. It's always been my practice to try to keep the camera upwind of the area I'm trying to photograph. I don't have the capability or wherewithal to make myself and the rest of my equipment scent-free, so I'm knowingly searching for Sasquatch with that handicap. It has also been suggested that the hairy fellow can sense the electromagnetic field or see the infrared light emitted from these devices.

It occurs to me that most proponents (opponents of trail cam methodology) of these hypotheses argue from a point of *single cause* or *false cause*. Fallaciously meaning: "If Bigfoot has never appeared on a trail-cam photo then the creature must know to avoid them." Such a statement neglects to acknowledge any number of other causes; the most likely of which is: maybe there just wasn't a Sasquatch in the area to trigger the camera trap.

Any wildlife is equipped to sense a man-made intrusion into their habitat. If you're going to use a trail-cam then be smart about it. You may want to set up the device in another location away from where you're conducting your primary investigation. I don't doubt that Sasquatch are intelligent. But I don't believe they know *what* a photograph *is* or what exactly that camera *does*. Dogs, for an admittedly morbid example, know what a car is and that they shouldn't get in front of a moving one. Unfortunately, from time to time a dog is either careless enough or just plain dumb enough to get hit by one. Someday, an equally careless (or dumb) Bigfoot is going to step in front of a trail-cam. It may as well be yours.

__Binoculars: I'm sure you understand this but a good set of field glasses helps with long-range identification. You may want to ere on the side of lightweight and compact as they do you little good if you're not willing to carry them.

__Bigfoot field guide or guidebook. Mine is good, Meldrum's is better.

__A card viewer or another method to view images on memory cards. There are small dongles[41] available for your phone and apps to aid in this. Test it first, the reader app and/or card reader may not work well with video files.

__Backup batteries for said electronics

__Evidence collection kit. As previously discussed, have tools and storage containers to collect physical evidence, like hairs. They need to be as-close-to-sterile as is possible.

---

[41] Ha! *Dongle*.

Secretly Seeking Sasquatch

__An item of *curiosity*. By many, many accounts Bigfoot seems to be as curious as any other primate. I routinely leave a baseball within view of my camera trap in hopes of getting Sasquatch to take the offering. Wouldn't it be great if he threw it at me later?! This comes from the *E.T.* school of interspecies communication.[42] You may consider a small toy or something shiny. As Derek Randles told me during an Olympic Mountains expedition, "it's thinking outside of the box that yields the best results."

Figure 30: Bait.

Money is no option...you have a rich benefactor funding your research efforts:

__Heat Imaging Camera
__Night Vision
__Parabolic Microphone
__Sherpas to pack and care for the llamas.
__Llamas to carry your gear.

Beyond all of these things and by far, the best thing you can bring with you into the field is a critical, yet open mind. Not every sound or blurry hair-covered

---

[42] E.T. The Extra-Terrestrial, Steven Spielberg, 1982

haunch viewed in hasty retreat is a Sasquatch. The term "trained observer" is often thrown around in fields delving into subject matter that are less-than-normal. When a police officer, park ranger, or soldier report a Sasquatch encounter, investigators take note. First off, they're supposed to be trustworthy. They've gone through a lot of interviews and processes to ensure their truthfulness. Secondly, their testimony could be golden because they've been trained to gather details even under physical or emotional duress, something not every citizen may be able to muster.

I sat in a cadet-filled classroom one early academy morning listening to a lecture by our commander on this very subject. Suddenly, an angry man burst through the door. He seemed very agitated and in his left hand, he held a hatchet. With the hatchet hand he pointed at the commander and said: "Overby, I'm tired of you parking in my damn parking space!" Commander Overby responded rather sheepishly and it was about three seconds, three VERY long seconds until I realized this was all an act, an exercise to drive home a point. The man, we later found out was the campus landscaper, Gary Nondorf. He apparently participated in this ruse every year and was quite good at it. After he left, of course, we were asked to write down everything we remembered about the occurrence. Most of us proved proficient at estimating his age, height, weight, and ethnicity as well as everything he was wearing. As the cadets joked about the startling incident at break time we added "and a big [expletive] ax!" The value of making observations, as experienced in my career, went well beyond these confrontational situations. You became good at gathering details because frankly, you were going to have to write a report on it later. I gravitate toward deputy Herrington's encounter (Green, The Best of Bigfoot Sasquatch, 2004) in Grays Harbor County for this reason because I consider him to have provided excellent witness testimony and garnered impeccable credibility due to his status as a trained observer.

There's a strange paradox often encountered with Bigfoot and how the media treats the report of a sighting. I'm reminded of some hullabaloo surrounding a psychologist and his Bigfoot sighting along a road in Oregon. The witness's Ph.D. was thrown around to support the credibility and earnestness of his statement. This is all well and good and, by all accounts, it's a very good sighting. But as Loren Coleman points out in *Bigfoot! The True Story of Apes in America*, "His sighting was taken seriously, although some within the Bigfoot study ranks were upset that the press would treat a Ph.D. so nobly when the media ignores reports from truck drivers, farmers, and hunters every week" (Coleman, 2004).

I'm going to deliberately make a generalization. So please, don't interpret this to mean I don't recognize hunting accidents or take them lightly. The hunter carries a tool which delivers a lethal projectile. The very first lesson the new hunter learns is what they're looking at and what they're about to shoot. How to tell a man from beast and male prey from female are lessons that weigh heavily because mistakes could cost a hunter their freedom and conscience in one tragic fell swoop. Advanced lessons include topography, geography, and how the creatures of the land think and act. A hunter should be an excellent judge of distance. They're even adept at judging the weather's cues. For these reasons, I believe hunters are trained observers and when it comes to the subject of Bigfoot, so long as the hunter-witness seems credible and his or her experience legitimate then a couple of "hey-this-person-may-really-be-telling-the-truth" points should be tacked on due to the fact that you can trust their observations. At the very least, they should be awarded the same benefit of the doubt as a physician, law officer, or clergyman.

The same inferences could be made about the farmer. In my early college years, I returned home for the summer and took up work on a wheat farm. Now, this is small-town charm at its best because my employer was the husband of my first-grade teacher. Don McHargue ran a family wheat farm and kept a heard of beef cattle. We'd be driving the gravel roads in a decades-old pickup truck. At any moment, at any pasture, any alfalfa flat or any random wheat slope, he could notice something *wrong*. It was like a sixth sense. Most often it was during calving season. He could spot a mother-to-be-bovine laying down or acting strange from literally hundreds of yards away. Sometimes the absence of the cow was enough to hit the brakes and nearly ditch the truck. Had a Bigfoot barged through his barley, he would have noticed for he was a trained observer.

Jason M. Burke

Pareidolia the Destroyer

As a child I spent many a summer week at my grandparents' home on the ranch. I'd sleep in their living on a hideaway couch made into a guest bed. Their living room walls were dressed in faux wood paneling. At night I'd lie in bed and stare at the simulated wood grain. An evil owl would stare back…menacingly. Was there really an owl? No. Was there a demonic presence communicating its ill intent devilishly to me, telepathically, and did my mind, struggling to define the event, merely assign the image of an owl to the scary events which scarred my psyche? Still no. The image of the owl was imagined. The alternating contrast of dark and light wooden swirls happened to resemble a particularly mischievous bird of prey. Those dots were connected in my mind. This is *pareidolia*.

It's what causes us to see the man in the moon, rocks that look like faces, and the last supper in a tortilla chip. Listen to a babbling brook or even a fish tank's air pump bubbling up through the water. Let your mind wander and you may be snapped to attention and swear you just heard a nearly inaudible conversation. This is but an auditory version of the same phenomenon.

In fact, just being able to recognize art, like a painting as a person or recognizing hand-drawn boat are examples of pareidolia in its most raw and primitive form.

Pareidolia runs rampant in a subject like Bigfoot just like it does in the ghost and UFO fields. Over-enthusiastic true-believers commonly squint at the pixels of a photo and enthusiastically point to the eerie or other-worldly visitor or even a Sasquatch photobomb. Depending on your emotional state, like-mindedness, or susceptibility to pareidolia, you too may see exactly what you're encouraged to see. Not unlike a Rorschach Test, observers can be tricked into recognizing ghostly faces from mere shadows and reflections just as one may recognize a butterfly in an inkblot. The condition undoubtedly discredits the field to some degree and it occurs on both ends of the spectrum with one end squinting out a zipper or wristwatch from the pixels as the other may be tricked into seeing anatomical Bigfoot hallmarks.

Figure 31: Ha! That's a polaroid of me at Grandma's house. Can you spot the owl in the paneling? Because I can't. I think it's blocked by my leg.

Consider this example: In my ranger days at the haunted seminary, we were often approached by ghost enthusiasts. They had questions and wanted access to the building. Above all, they wanted some sort of admission from me, a government official. Most times they were met with my dismissive denial for two main reasons: 1. I didn't want to deal with late-night break-ins from would-be ghost hunters and 2. I didn't feel qualified to comment on the subject. We would give tours if they were scheduled ahead of time and one day, I gave a tour to two ladies. Now, I kind of feel slated as their true intent wasn't stated upfront but this pair represented (as this was later revealed) the Washington Ghost Society. In the days after the tour, our office received several calls wanting to schedule a ghost investigation. It was an unusual request but, aside from having to work extra late on the night in question, there was really no reason to turn them down. The crew that showed up that night consisted of about a dozen people and they split into teams. Each team consisted of an equipment technician (who operated cameras, electromagnetic field detectors, and digital sound recorders), an investigator, and a *psychic*. I've italicized psychic and please let me explain before your ectoplasm begins to boil. I am completely open to the idea of ESP[43]. I myself have had a few incidences of profound Deja vu accompanied by an eerie, seemingly prophetic dream. I'm not claiming to be the next Nostradamus or to have returned from Steven King's *Dead Zone*, I'm just optimistic we'll learn much more about this phenomenon as scientists continue to unlock the secrets of the human mind. THAT BEING SAID, without any sort of proof to offer, I'm a hard-nosed agnostic if someone tells me they're a psychic. What I saw that night was a bunch of adults walking around using their imaginations. I'm not trying to poo-poo all of ghost research. I'm not even saying that all of what I witnessed that night was bunk. I'm just saying that someone standing in, what is clearly an empty cafeteria, telling me they sense "warm meals and comradery," falls well short of definitive proof. So much of the ghost hunt that long, late night, regrettably, was colored by me quoting *Ghostbusters* and *Poltergeist* lines to elicit a laugh from Mohammad. When the investigation was over, some weeks later, we met with two of the lead investigators from the crew. Admittedly, these guys were respectable and professional. Apparently, the ghost society has just about the same balance of well-meaning (and well-grounded) people and kooks as the Sasquatch spectrum does. We were presented with some photographs, some video, and a few compelling sound recordings. If you're not familiar with the EVP phenomenon, it would seem some ghostly voices, inaudible at the time and captured on a digital sound recorder, can be heard later at an amplified volume. Researchers ask questions and are unable to hear any response at the time yet, it would seem, someone (or something) is answering the question on the recording. One EVP we were presented with was in response to the question "did you like living here?" The answer was a ghostly and resounding "Nooooo!" I'm just reporting the facts to you, this is what I was presented with and what I heard on the recording. My assessment of the photos varied from recognizing an admittedly ghostly image to seeing nothing at all or feeling that the image was most likely an old pareidolia mind-trick. In one such image, taken in the infrared spectrum, shows the unlit chapel. Because of the setting, it is bathed in an eerie greenish hue. The greenish

---

[43] *Extrasensory perception*

hue seems quite pixelated and gives the impression of a felt-like texture. Let's call this texture "noise." If you stare at the noise long enough you can kind of see a man's face, transparent and ghostly. In yet another photo, this one taken in a standard setting, you can see a mist appearing midway down a long hallway. Whether it's a photo fluke, an atmospheric anomaly, or really a phantom mist, I don't know but it is there. Pareidolia encourages your mind to assign it a recognizable shape. I, for example, see a formless wisp but my sister claims to see a kneeling nun wearing a habit. So, interpretation, especially concerning pareidolia, is in the eye of the beholder.

I tell you this because simply being aware of it is a step in the right direction. Understanding what tricks your eyes, ears, and mind can play, will help to rule them out later in hopes of presenting your evidence and strengthening your argument. Remember, not every brownish, slightly humanoid blob is a Bigfoot and not every burned-out stump is a Sasquatch. I suppose you can say that in the other direction as well.

Figure 32: Can you see Bigfoot's face? Located along a trail on Mount Saint Helens' south side.

Bigfoot: How I see Him/Her/It/Them

It would seem to be universally agreed upon that Sasquatch has two hands and two feet with 5 digits on each appendage[44]. They have a mouth, fingernails, and toenails and are they are mostly covered in hair. They have a nose for breathing and teeth for eating. They have two eyes facing forward in their heads. There are males and there are females. Children have been seen ranging from infants to adolescents. They eat. They poop.

Based on what I understand about evolution this describes a creature that evolved here on Earth. They seem to be completely suited for the climate and environment in which they are most commonly reported.

Here are the Sasquatch truths as I see them:

Positive vibes, baby: You have a better chance of seeing one if your intentions and demeanor are non-threatening. If you were to approach a stray pet or a wild animal (unadvisable under most circumstances) you wouldn't go in aggressively, acting unpredictably or using a loud or gruff voice. It is human nature and common sense to approach slowly, with a soft voice, kindly and gently. I'm not saying you'll approach Bigfoot but I am saying this technique also subconsciously projects a harmless intent. There are pheromones and subtle body

---

[44] There are anomalies, though infrequent, ranging from 3 to six toes documented from footprints. Causes, if from a Sasquatch, could range from missing toes, toes that just didn't copy into the footprint, birth defects, polydactylism or even mutations brought on by inbreeding. Some of these reports are accompanied by strange occurrences that may well fall outside the Bigfoot realm. For this reason I suggest Peter Guttilla's *The Bigfoot Files* for further reading.

language cues of which you're not even aware. If your intentions are aggressive or overly fearful, you'll project those invisible signs as well.

Leave the stealth on the shelf: You're not going to sneak up on one. I believe their senses are just too sharp and attuned. You do have a chance of "stumbling" upon one. Perhaps near a loud river where one is crouched behind a boulder or you're lucky enough to drive up on a road crossing.

Be interesting: Sing. Laugh. Talk in a conversational voice. Appear interesting. If a Sasquatch is watching, you're the TV show. Curiosity on the part of the watcher gives you the advantage of drawing it closer and possibly stepping out for a moment.

Good or Bad? A large group of experiencers and believers preach that these creatures are gentle giants and the kind guardians of the forest. Others, some of whom I know, report terrifying encounters of being chased and intimidated. One cannot apply either trait, broad-brushed, to the entire population. Think about dogs. There are kind dogs that would lead the burglar to the jewelry safe for a good pat on the head or throwing of the ball. There are also dogs that will chase you at a speed of 43 miles per hour as you try to bike past their house. Dog personalities (training aside) run the entire gambit. If you look at a population of intelligent animals, you're bound to find the same range of behavioral trait variances. Motivation in a single Sasquatch would likely vary too. A person who witnessed one kind forest giant simply doesn't have the sample size to accurately anthropomorphize an entire species.

Advice to a Noob from an Intermediate Noob

Bigfoot expert? I'm not even a self-proclaimed expert! I'm not even sure what a *Bigfoot expert* is. There are certainly people with advanced degrees in anthropology, zoology, anatomy, and biology and there are wildlife biologists, expert trackers and world travelers with ape experience who are contributing to the field.

Those who have worked in this field for multiple decades have probably studied with the likes of John Green, Rene' Dahinden, Peter Byrne, Cliff Crook, Grover Krantz, Dr. John Bindernagel, Ivan Sanderson, Dr. Jeff Meldrum, Bob Gimlin and Roger Patterson (did I forget anybody?). Certainly, given this resume', it would be excusable for adopting the title of Bigfoot expert, if only honorary. Truthfully with no corpse to autopsy, bones from which to reconstruct a skeleton, or, especially, a living specimen to observe for a long period of time, there are no (known) bona fide Bigfoot experts.

I've shared my mistakes and I've learned from them. Sometimes I've even repeated a mistake or two (which I realize implies I *didn't* learn from them). I haven't seen a Sasquatch. In my travels, there have been experiences that are consistent with Bigfoot activity.[45]

On two occasions immediately upon arrival to a *Bigfoot area*, I've heard an extremely loud limb snap. One happened precisely as Lori and I exited the car. This was accompanied by a wood knock[46]. The second occasion occurred in

---

[45] I make no claims that these are definitively evidence of Bigfoot. I'm attempting to objectively share experiences with you that seemed unusual at the time that occurred in areas where Sasquatch reports have been reported for decades.

[46] Experiencers and many researchers hypothesize that Bigfoot use a limb or a rock to strike a tree or stump to make a loud, resounding "wood knock" sound. Rock to

southwestern Washington. Adam and I had driven along a river up a forest road near Lake Cushman. We decided to get out of the car in a clear cut. As we approached the timberline, we heard a very loud limb-snap. These are personal impressions. I can't say that "coincidence" has any scientific bearing but the noises, on both occasions, *felt* deliberate and occurred as we approached. In either event, we saw no other people or cars.

I believe the print I found near Quilcene to be authentic, that is, consistent with prints reportedly left behind by the Sasquatch creature. It was far from a perfect print. I cannot rule out another type of track. Hoaxing seems unlikely as it would be very unlikely to be discovered in that location. The tree breaks, an oft-reported hallmark of Bigfoot activity, cued me in on the track find.

In the northern Cascades, where a muddy creek crosses the trail, there were many large, yet very anomalous tracks. For all I know, they could've been human boot prints. While examining the prints though, and walking deeper into the woods near a waterfall, I heard a very distinct *tongue click*, the popping sound you can make by snapping your tongue downward from the roof of your mouth. Again, given the absence of other people and cars, human contamination seems unlikely.

The buttprint (as you'll read in the Walla Walla chapter) in the dry gravelly dust is an enigma. It serves as a shining example of how I should've measured it in the photo. It looks as I'd expect a Sasquatch butt print to look. There were no other prints to corroborate this hypothesis.

Lastly, while at the Olympic Project's public expedition I heard a howl. I grew up in coyote country so I'm ready to dismiss coyotes outright. I've heard one wolf in the wild, in addition to what I've heard on television. The noise did not have canine qualities that I've ever heard. It was a howl and not within the barred owl's repertoire. I can't rule out common forest animals of which I'm unfamiliar. It did, however, sound similar to sound recordings that David Ellis has in his audio library. These sounds defy explanation and, as of right now, are believed to have come from Sasquatch. It occurred just after 3 a.m. Cliff Barackman was in attendance for this particular expedition. He had led a night outing but this had been over for several hours. Simply put, everyone had gone to bed. The temperature was below freezing and the noise originated to the west which was deeper into the mountains. For this reason, I believe I can rule out a noise made by a human.

---

rock strikes are also reported. Most recently I've heard a hypothesis that many of these wood knocking sounds could be loud clapping caused by two, very large Sasquatch hands. Wood knocks are easily fouled by human interaction via wood-splitting and, of course, other people striking trees with limbs and baseball bats.

Sasquatch Sins

I may not have a Sasquatch carcass in my freezer or even part of one for that matter. I have, however, been an excellent observer and a student of human foibles. Here is a list of the gaffes that drive me crazy.

There's no way a human could have done THAT: Under most circumstances, ruling out human interference is almost impossible. Certainly, if you see a Sasquatch beyond a mere glimpse and within a reasonable distance, you'd feel confident saying that there was no way it was a man in a suit. But that's not what I'm talking about here. I'm cautioning you against reading too much into stick structures and other seemingly non-natural phenomena that appear in the woods.

At a conference, I spoke to a very kind woman who was exuberantly excited to discuss her findings of Bigfoot "glyphs." It was her belief she was finding

Figure 33: Alleged glyph from SW Washington.

symbols, made by Sasquatch, spelled out on the ground in a mountainous area she frequents.

She closed with the qualifier: "there's no way a human would have done that." Well, yes, a person very well could have. When we're talking stick structures and, especially rock-stacking or glyphs, it is very hard to rule out human hands at play. Kids build stick lean-twos and people seem to have an intrinsic need to stack rocks. Also consider, if your defense is "no one goes up there," my response would be YOU go up there so it must have some appeal. Stick structures are a commonly accepted piece of Bigfoot evidence but you need to dig up some corroborative evidence before you jump to "what else could it be?" This is ten years of park rangering talking: people do some weird stuff. Furthermore, boulders can roll into trails and trees can naturally blow over into teepee shapes. I have no statistical data for this statement, but as a tree-felling ranger, I feel that, at least in the woods I worked in, a failing tree was as likely to get hung up in another tree as it was to hit the ground flat.

Here again, in my experience, overpopulated and undernourished alder forests seemed to produce natural teepees (treepees?).

Figure 34: A second glyph.

Figure 35: Behold! The stump of the googly eyes! People do some weird things. Photo of author by Scott Robinson.

Failing Fallacies: It has been a long time since junior college sociology.[47] Undoubtedly, I have committed more than one fallacy in my conversation with you. My advice though, however hypocritical, is to avoid fallacies in your discussions concerning Sasquatch. In the preceding example, I believe the nice woman, albeit innocently, defended her evidence with the fallacy of *hasty generalization*. In short, it involves jumping to a conclusion and not considering all of the evidence. There are gaps between the premise and the conclusion. Chad Arment brilliantly discusses fallacies as they pertain to cryptozoology, and especially Sasquatch in *Cryptozoology Science and Speculation* (pp. 38-55). I share this because you may eventually find yourself defending a hypothesis, presenting a piece of evidence, or engaging in a spirited debate. You'll maintain credibility, not to mention firmer footing, if you don't do so from a slippery slope.

The "They:" "I thought *they* proved that all to be a fake" and "*They* know about it; they're just trying to cover it up" are both over-generalized statements I've encountered in my research on both far opposing ends of the spectrum.

Who are the *they*?

The prior statement came from a very intelligent, yet unworldly former ranger boss of mine from the Olympic Peninsula. During a spirited lunchtime discussion about Bigfoot, he parried with what I believe he thought as a debate ending rebuttal. "But Jason, I thought *they* proved that all to be fake." I have often

---

[47] Go North Idaho College Cardinals!

encountered the enigmatic "they," a group of ill-defined people or an organization dedicated to winning an argument without citing any sources or providing any facts. This wasn't the first time I'd the run afoul of the *they* but it was the first time I asked: "who's the *they* in that sentence?" He stammered on a bit, first it was the news…then a documentary then, simply a show that "proved" Bigfoot to be a hoax by way of discrediting the Patterson-Gimlin Film (PGF). His rebuttal was rife with fallacies but I was kind and simply explained that the show in-question presented a supposed confession wherein Bob Hieronimus (a man with legitimate ties to Patterson and Gimlin) "admitted" to being "the man in the suit." I let him have this one. I wasn't energetic or prepared enough to debate the PGF at that time but I did point out the fallacious assumption that just because one piece of film evidence was "proven[48]" fake doesn't discount, discredit, or disprove the entire phenomenon. He actually courteously considered my point of view as something he hadn't considered previously. This was a time before Facebook…a time when a person could "win" an argument.

The latter statement I've encountered on numerous occasions on numerous subjects. "They know about it; they're just trying to cover it up." This leads us down an even more devious and darker rabbit hole and it's harder to shed light on what it is the person is really trying to say.

While I don't subscribe to most fringe theories and conspiratorial dogma, I'm not naïve. There *are, have been,* and *will be* cover-ups by organizations we trust, or, at a minimum, should be able to trust. The danger, I feel, is anthropomorphizing an entire group to presume duplicitous intent. Something akin to treating "the government" as a devious person. Doing so is contaminated with fallacy and has limitless potential for paranoia. If you don't trust the government because they're coveting knowledge of extraterrestrial visitation…then where do you draw the line? Is your letter carrier in on it? The airman at the front gate? The TSA?

Don't read the comments: There are trolls lurking under every social media bridge and the toll will cost you your dignity and confidence. I started *Secretly Seeking Sasquatch*[49] as a means to share my photos, adventures and, eventually to promote my book. My following is teetering just under a very meager 1000 followers. Fortunately, this seems to be so low as to be off the trolls' collective RADAR as it has not been a problem. I was naïve at first. I felt that if I caught a really good video or an excellent piece of forensic evidence that sharing on social

---

[48] Understand, I don't feel this alleged confession proves anything. There's a disparaging tendency for interested parties to believe these assertions outright coming from individuals who suspiciously throw themselves into the fray. I'd ask the reader to look into the PGF themselves and reach their own conclusions.

[49] Secretly Seeking Sasquatch: www.facebook.com/washingtongieldguide/

media would equate to peer review, a crucial step in the scientific method. No. At least "no" in the sense of just throwing it out there. You're the most vulnerable if you post something within the comments of another researcher's post. For those who ravenously follow Sasquatch in the digital realm, most are from the extreme ends, neither of whom are very objective or open-minded. As I'm sure you've noticed by now, this person is the most likely to air their beliefs and promote their dogma. The 100% true-believer is already convinced and a poor source of objectivity and the cynical skeptics are just there to mock. There is even a strange sub-culture of self-proclaimed Bigfoot experts who will tell you you're wasting your time based on x, y, and z. They won't be nice, either. This doesn't mean you shouldn't participate. If you're going to share though, find a reputable researcher and private message or email them. Assemble your presentation intelligently, objectively, and avoid fallacies.

The best defense is no defensiveness: If you've laid it all out there on social media then: good luck. There are those who may defend you but mostly, you're on your own. Try not to take it personally. This is a good segue into a piece of advice: Should you share a piece of evidence, usually a photo or perhaps you're telling of a sighting or experience, don't get defensive when you start to hear hypotheses contrary to your own. A footprint find will be extraordinary but mostly just to you. A single footprint will hardly be enough to get a researcher with a Ph.D. on a plane to fly out to your site. A trackway or forensic evidence with a sighting, however, is a different thing altogether. You also should be prepared to hear what you don't necessarily want to hear. Something to the tune of "that's a human footprint" or "that's likely a bear print within a bear print." My advice is don't take it personally and don't get defensive. That's not to say you can't defend your supposition but do so under what would be considered respectful debate protocol and use as many facts as you can in defense of your claim.

Shaky chain of evidence: A court would never allow a piece of key evidence to be submitted with a questionable evidence chain. Many a video is presented by someone distantly separated from the witness who inevitably remains anonymous whereby damaging its credibility.

"After the fact" or "discovered later": It's entirely possible that Bigfoot did photobomb your family reunion. It had better be a pretty convincing piece of photographic or video evidence, though, because hoaxers have mined this area pretty heavily with the "it wasn't until I loaded the images onto the computer that I noticed…" setup.

One single photo: The proponent of the photo boasts evidence that will "end all skepticism" and "undeniably prove Bigfoot to the world." Then why just the one photo? What you see is a brown amorphous blob that is likely a burnt-out tree stump. I've seen many animal "shapes" from trail cameras. The ones I find the most suspect are the single suspect frame. Very likely there are photos leading into the mystery one and photos after. Any photo, even if you believe it to be "empty" could reveal a clue. Often times this is why the proponent neglects to share more photos. Consider this: you set up your trail cam and after reviewing the photo card you see three photos of bears, an amorphous hairy appendage that could be a Sasquatch's arm and then 2 more photos of bears. I'm not saying Bigfoot wasn't there but if you don't share the bear photos too, you're being deceptive.

One footprint, no scale: Is it possible that you will only find a single, solitary Sasquatch print? Yes. Too many times though, there's but a single photograph with no indication of scale. In this day there's no such thing as wasting film. Also, your foot is a poor indicator of scale. "My size 13 boot next to the print." I'll concede, that this is better than nothing but you're then obligated to measure your boot once you get home and I've, not once, seen this type of follow-through.

Wally, the Wildman of Walla Walla, Washington

Even if "Wally" isn't the official nickname of Walla Walla's wood-ape, it should be (or Wanda in the case of a female). Walla Walla, the Blue Mountains, and the Umatilla National Forest were a frustrating conundrum for me. The area seemed controversial and largely inaccessible. I grew up in Eastern Washington and beyond Basketball bus trips (I was in the band), I hadn't spent much time there so I formed the erroneous assumption that it was all rolling grain crops and rangeland. The agricultural environment is very familiar to me and it was hard to imagine Sasquatch occupying the mountains so close to combines and cows.

The Blues have their pages in Sasquatch lore, much of which is focused around one man. Paul Freeman (now deceased) claimed to have seen Bigfoot on numerous occasions, found and cast several prints, and allegedly caught Sasquatch on film in what is now known as "The Freeman Video." Too good to be true? This is the filter that has been used to discredit many witnesses and contributors in the cryptozoological field. Roger Patterson and Bob Gimlin were passed through the same thresher when their famous film sensationalized the creature and polarized the population largely into two camps: believers and skeptics. Opponents squawked *how convenient it is that two cowboys looking for and filming a Sasquatch documentary manage to capture one on film!* My interpretation here is intentionally glib but my point is, there's a mentality out there that evidence submitted by Bigfoot investigators will be more severely scrutinized based solely on the fact that they've dedicated their time, finances, and in some cases, their lives, to search for Bigfoot. If someone cries HOAX, it's nearly impossible to recover.

    To some degree, Freeman was to the 1990s what Patterson and Gimlin were to the '60s. What was different, was America's interest in tabloids and sensational controversy-fueled television like *Hardcopy*. The media wasn't always kind to witnesses and seemed to prey on those who may have, let's say *unique* personalities. The internet was still a few years off and I feel the general public was much more trusting of what they read in newspapers and saw on television than they are today. So, if a journalist treated a Bigfoot sighting in a less-than-positive fashion, the general public was inclined to accept the sarcasm as canon. Freeman wasn't one to shy away from the media's attention. As a forest employee, Freeman had the distinction of knowing the lay of the land and spending a great deal of time there. He claimed to have had numerous sightings and was able to produce casts of footprints, handprints, and even a buttprint. Some in the field felt he was suspiciously too lucky but some took notice when Dr. Jeff Meldrum announced that a few of the footprint casts displayed dermal ridges, fingerprints of a sort, pointing to the existence of the living, breathing unknown primate who made them. Furthermore, Meldrum maintains that the prints he cast, with Freeman present, demonstrated telltale traits you'd expect to find from authentic prints. The toes splayed to grip the ground in places and the flesh of a soft foot-shaped around rocks the creature had stepped on, something a homemade prosthesis was unlikely to do (M20).

    Freeman had supporters and opponents within his own Bigfoot community. It has been suggested, that Freeman even faked evidence. This even caused me to sort of camp out in the distrustful side of the spectrum but I began to reconsider this notion after I attended a presentation by a long-time Bigfoot researcher and *Finding Bigfoot* staff member. His explanation for Freeman's dreaded hoaxer reputation stemmed from an interview where Freeman was asked if he ever made a Sasquatch footprint, meaning an artificial representation of one. Freeman said yes and went on to explain that is was in the name of research and he wanted to see how truly easy, or not, such a thing would be for someone to hoax. This confession, according to the speaker, was taken out of context and spun negatively by the media sources.

Hearsay? Yes. But I mention this so as to help you understand my conundrum concerning my treatment of the Walla Walla area. If you discard Paul Freeman, you throw out a lot Bigfoot evidence.

So, I'm going to choose to trust Paul Freeman. I'm going to give him the benefit of the doubt and I'm not going to rake a deceased man over the coals. I encourage you to view the Freeman footage for yourself and look at the bigger picture, taking anything you read with a grain of salt. Paul Freeman aside, other people have recorded encounters with the man-ape near the towns of Walla Walla (M20) and Dayton (M21). It's a phenomenon I feel is more sewn into the local lore than what is evident in any online database.

Bigfoot is here, somewhere. The trick is getting there. Leaving Seattle I racked well over a thousand miles and trashed my poor Focus. I grew up on a farm located on a rural gravel road and I don't remember dust like this. I could have bagged the silty loam that settled inside my car and sold it at some hipster urban farmer's market as a garden amendment. The area is dusty, rough, remote, and difficult to access. You may have to endure such personal hazards as snakes and ticks. Difficult but not impossible.

So, I'm going to stray a bit from my mantra: "these routes should be within the abilities of an average family sedan." This one is a little rough but worth your time. If you have a pickup or a beat-up sedan, then get out there and explore the

Blue Mountains. Your lowered Nissan Stanza isn't going to make it though. I went on a weekend in early July and saw less than a dozen people. Don't go during hunting season unless you're hunting or are particularly fond of Carhartt's and hunter's orange. I found that most of the areas on the western slopes of the Blues, just outside of Walla Walla are private property, fields, and rangeland. So, please don't trespass. But if you favor beautiful photo ops and a nice, albeit rocky, mountain drive then give Biscuit and Blacksnake Ridge (M20) a shot.

A slightly more explorative approach departs from Dayton (M21). Take the N. Fork Touchet River Road into the Umatilla National Forest. Shortly after a ski and recreation area, the paved road will turn to gravel and then dirt. The biggest challenge was getting my car up over the water bars[50] without bottoming out and/or getting high centered. I never got stuck nor was I in any real danger of that. I did, however, bottom out a couple of times and there were often large rocks in the road. The route I've provided takes you up to Kendall Skyline Road. If you kept trekking on, you'd cross into Oregon. This was my intent as I drove and drove. I wanted to make it to Deduct Springs, the sight of where Freeman shot his Bigfoot footage (Meldrum pp. 128-131). For the sake of my car's struts, I stopped about 5 miles short of the state line. I found a spring-fed creek and saw many animal prints. There was a high concentration of elk and deer prints and it was obvious that this was a place where animals congregated for a cool drink and some shady damp ground to escape the summer heat. I found one print peculiar. There were three deep indentations resembling toes and two shallower indentations. I wouldn't go so far as to call this a "footprint" but there were 5 indentations, perhaps tiny deer hoofmarks. But maybe these were giant finger or toe indentations. Having learned from my first evidence-collecting blunder I decided to go ahead and document the print thoroughly. I took photos, with the tape measure in view thinking "I don't need to write these measurements down, they're on the photo!" I then, subsequently, managed to delete these photos by inadvertently swapping SDHC cards with my trail cam. So, all my photos and "ingenious" digital notes were reduced to electronic oblivion. And yes, "Electronic Oblivion" would be an awesome name for a band. Feel free to use it.

Then I talked myself into casting the *print*. I wasn't at all convinced this was a Sasquatch print but with my previous mistake still burning freshly in my mind, I talked myself into casting it. When in doubt, CAST IT. I got my Bigfoot kit and commenced covering my hands, arms, face, slower-moving squirrels, and

---

[50] A sort of speedbump-shaped hump built to divert water to the side of the road rather than allow it to flow like a stream down the center of the road.

sandwiches with wet white plaster. Then I poured what remained into my phantom print.

I hadn't seen a living soul sans bird and chipmunk all day when about this time a kindly, retirement-aged couple (in their early 70's) happened to drive by in a Chevy Trailblazer. Bear in mind, they've happened upon a 2wd commuter car high in the wilds of the Umatilla, in the middle of July and just encountered a man covered in a pasty white substance, sweating profusely.

Their truck slowed, stopped and the driver's side window descended with an electronic whir. Cool, conditioned air escaped the vehicle.

"Whatcha doing?" the man said. There was an air of cautious jest in his voice as though he thought, should this conversation turn sour, he and his wife could end up in a barrel labeled "torsos" by the end of the day.

"I'm casting a print" I replied, in a reassuring voice, as one might use with a baby animal.

"Oh!" he said relieved. "Are you doing a study?"

"No. I'm writing a Bigfoot book and I found what looks like it could be a three or five-toe track."

The air of caution returned. The vehicle inched forward but stopped again.

The couple chatted me up a bit and commented on the large elk herd known to inhabit the Umatilla Wilderness. As they slowly rolled down the mountain road, the man's parting salutation to me was "Later dude." Now, "dude" doesn't enter into a 70-year-old man's vocabulary unless it is used to condescendingly address an unkempt teenager or to say goodbye to someone, who very well could be, suffering from a severe chemical imbalance bordering on dementia.

But my point isn't really about the ambiguous undocumented mystery print. Waiting for my plaster to dry, I explored the area looking for correlating sign I hiked up to the ridgeline. It was rocky and dry here and, in the soil, I saw a butt print. Yes, it looked like the impression someone's buttocks and thighs would make if they sat upon the dusty soil (see photo). It was huge though, and I estimated it was about as wide as a standard interior door frame in a house. Meaning, if this was Aunt Bertha's rear, she'd have to turn sideways to get from the kitchen to the living room.

Almost, in passing afterthought, I snapped a photo of the print and moved on. Later when I would share my evidence and subsequent ineptitude with Dr. Meldrum. He replied (via email) with "Butt print interesting. Scale would have been nice." Meaning, if you're going to take the time to document something photographically, you may as well measure it or, at a minimum, include something of known size for scale. Another lesson learned.

Figure 36: Buttprint? It was high up in the Blues above the Touchet River.

Jason M. Burke

The Rabbit Hole

Go ask Alice, when she's ten feet tall.

-Jefferson Airplane

I stood upon a black hole in the forest. A weathered wooden sign above the hole read simply "Bigfoot." I knew the hole was deep, but I had no way of knowing how deep. I knew the hole was scary but there was no way for me to understand how scary. There was no way I could even fathom the array of characters I would encounter within. Some delightful and trustworthy. Others, dark, deceitful and self-serving. For better or worse, I closed my eyes extended my leg and tumbled into the abyss.

If your interest in the Bigfoot world piqued during adulthood then this analogy should ring true, it was a door you had to walk through into a room filled with mysterious characters and creatures of horror and delight.

My point is, the deeper I went, the stranger the story got. I've met wonderful people and I've encountered pathetic trolls. The community has, just like religion and politics, two extreme ends. Representatives from each end don't get along well. Many are like me and don't enjoy the infighting.

I've shown you where the rabbit hole is. I've attempted to give you a list of some recommendations and precautions that will aide in your tumble. If it's your agenda or practice to attack others solely based on the reason that they believe differently than you do, then I have no time for you.

I befriended many people on this road of mine and, while on an expedition in southwest Washington I met several people, both researchers, and witnesses, that have a much more extensive and respectful dossier in this field than I. It was around the campfire in a notorious Sasquatch haunt that stories were shared.

These were stories that I was unprepared to hear and, up until this point, I was unwilling to consider. These storytellers had shone their flashlights much deeper into the rabbit hole. I'm speaking about Adam and Nadia who I mentioned earlier. Adam recounted the tale with some emotion and difficulty in the telling, that had occurred during what was supposed to be a Sasquatch outing. Something *else* happened. The event was witnessed by four people. Adam and a close friend had the most direct contact with these *beings*, an encounter that turned into a conflict. Two strange creatures tormented the men that night. The encounter happened in a place that is definitely wired for weird. The antagonists weren't men or hoaxers nor was it some sort of light and hologram show. These creatures weren't of the Bigfoot variety. These things were terrifying, defied physics as we understand it, and exuded malicious intent. I cannot explain further. It is Adam's story to tell. You can easily find one of his podcast interviews. I would plead with you to listen to Adam and his close friend first. In at least one instance, they're interviewed together. The other witness (and the fourth, his son) has a different *interpretation*. If you pursue this matter, look into Adam's account first.

I respect these individuals. They gave me no reason to distrust their word or their judgment. They accepted risk in sharing with me these accounts but placed faith in me that I wouldn't attack their character or their word.

***

One of the worst thing that social media gave us was anonymity, a virtual wall where bullies could hide and hurl eggs. While many, many Bigfoot enthusiasts flock to the blogsites and social media pages to simply discuss, share, debate and learn, there are others who just want to argue, fight and tear others down personally. You would think it's just the skeptics or non-believers vs. the collective Bigfoot community, but it's not just that. The flesh-and-blooders fight the mystical Bigfoot types[51] and vice versa. This is unfortunate. The two groups may be sitting in the extreme opposite left and right ends of the boat but they ARE in the same proverbial boat.

Bigfoot to me is still a biological creature who is just as vulnerable to the laws of physics that we, you and me, are. This is still what I choose to believe. But I'm not as certain as I was before. There is something lurking there in the dark just out of the reach of my flashlight.

---

[51] Often referred to as "The Woo."

Jason M. Burke

The Search for Us

Reality is an illusion. The universe is a hologram. Buy gold. Bye!

-Bill Cipher, 'Gravity Falls,' Disney XD

The search for Bigfoot is the search for ourselves. The search for humanity. Now, this is cliché, flowery and deliberately contemplative, but it's true. And, yes, there are probably at least a dozen Bigfoot books that make the same comparison but if we suddenly found a giant previously undiscovered ape specimen in North America, living or dead, things would change overnight. It would also, however, only threaten our science and theology if we let it. If received with the proper attitude and open-minds, the discovery of such a creature could only expand upon our understanding of science and theology and, harmoniously, ourselves. We'll have discovered a previously unpublished chapter in *what it means to be human.*

Maybe I'm chasing a phantom. Maybe I'm looking for a shadow, an instinctual remnant, a creature that only exists as a memory in scraps of my prehistoric genes. Perhaps Sasquatch's reality to me exists merely because millions of years ago my ancestors shared the world with such a beast the same way they did with mastodons and saber-tooth cats. But I don't think so.

I simply can't accept that every single witness who shared their story was either lying, hoaxed, or mistaken. If only 1% of accounts remain after the previous three disqualifiers, then what exactly did the 1% see? Did their prehistoric intuition somehow trigger a bona fide hallucination? I don't think so.

Was it this same type of phantom mirage that caused me to see a green-glowing *something* in the bedroom closet of my home? Was it a dream that lingered in my brain seconds after I'd opened my eyes? I don't believe it was. I *know* what

I *saw*. This is a phrase that has been offered in rebuttal to critical skeptics of an eye-witness' account: "I know what a bear looks like and it wasn't a man in a suit. I know what I saw."

I didn't mention this earlier but I told my account of the glowing green phantom to Mohammad. I set it up very gravely with substantial qualifiers so there was no mistaking my sincerity and truthfulness in what I had experienced. I was expecting skepticism and even good-natured ribbing. What I heard in return was astounding. A number of months before, he'd been up at midnight and looked out his living room window (we lived in the same historic park building). Between the swimming pool building and Seminary, at about second-floor height, he saw a floating, glowing green orb! There are times my friend exaggerates but I know him nearly as well as his family does. This was not one of those times. He had seen the same thing I had. On this, I can say I know there's a greenish, glowing phenomenon with eerie properties that can only be described as *ghostly*.

Sadly, as far as Bigfoot is concerned, I cannot say that I know they exist. I don't know. I haven't seen one. For me, seeing is believing. I'm just wired with an agnostic brain, I guess. There are plenty of things in the world I haven't *seen* but I accept their existence because their existence is universally accepted. Sasquatch, for now, is a leap of faith…a question of whether or not you believe. Efforts to prove Sasquatch's existence are daunting at best. It occurs to me though, that it'd be astronomically easier to prove that a modern race of man-apes does exist than prove they don't. That kernel of possibility is enough for me. For this reason, I choose to believe. I also believe that a contingent of the reported encounters by witnesses is genuine. I believe that a portion of the footprints, hair samples, and other signs are also genuine. I lack the authority and qualifications to even estimate how much of the evidence and how many of the sightings are likely to be *genuine*, that is those that do not qualify as a lie, hoax, or mistake. I'm not sure it matters. The day Bigfoot is proven to be real will be the day that those statistics become irrelevant. If I see one, I may not be able to prove it to others but at least I'll know.

Henry Jones Sr. (Sean Connery) lie dying of a gunshot wound in a shrine built to hide the Holy Grail. The antagonist and traitor, Walter Donovan challenges Indiana Jones to retrieve the grail, whose purported miraculous powers can save his father's life. To bait Indy, he says "It's time to ask yourself *what* you *believe.*" Indy must then take a leap of faith (first figuratively then literally). You know how it ends and I'm in no mood to use the term SPOILER ALERT. A little faith and mystery were all Indy needed to go that extra step in search of the truth. I'm not likening myself to Indiana Jones, mind you (although I did dress like him on no fewer than seven separate Halloween gatherings). What I'm saying is, it's the mystery that interests me and the faith that compels me to attempt to solve the mystery myself. I'm in search of the truth. Bigfoot is out there somewhere. You can find him if you're lucky enough. This is what I choose to believe.

Imagine your most trusted confidant came to you with an amazing story. An 8-foot tall, 2-legged *something* had watched them while they picked huckleberries. You've never seen a Bigfoot and maybe you're even a staunch skeptic to boot. Your companion would never lie to you though. This you know. They're not gullible, it's hard to believe they could be hoaxed. What's left? To question their judgment or sanity?

It's time to ask yourself what you believe.

The Maps

I spent as much time drawing these maps as I did writing the book. I wanted hand-drawn maps, not just cut and paste Google Earth images. Of course, as you can tell they have an air of antiquity, like a treasure map or a mariner's map full of hazards and beasties. So, while they are a novelty, they're still useful. Growing up, long before GPS and smartphones, if you were lost, you asked directions. Often times, the kindly store clerk or farmer would draw you a map. It wouldn't be to scale but it would get you there.

Annnnnnnnnd then, after about 10 drafts of each map and three years of tinkering, I went entirely digital. There are probably those of you reading this that thought "awww…he made those in Photoshop. Not very good, though… *grumble*"

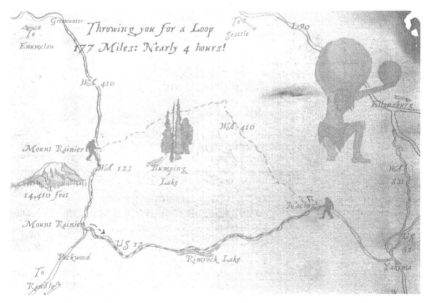

Figure 37: A discarded map, riddled with scanner flare.

These are as close-to-scale as I could manage. The dotted-route is measured in miles and this is very close to what a professional map would provide. Of course, the sketches and beasts are not to scale.

These maps are made to give you a fun adventure. They are not for survival purposes. So, use your head. Supplement your drive with GPS if you should feel so inclined. Practical directions are included with each map for this reason. Have fun and be careful. I used Google Maps to provide master keys to assist you.

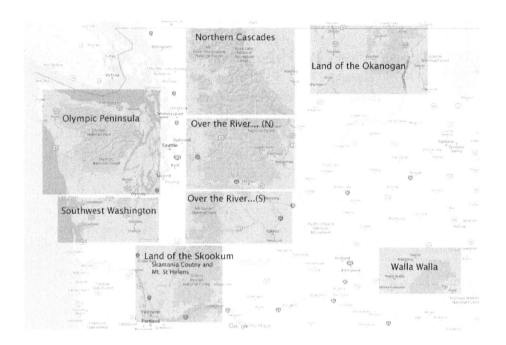

The Olympic Peninsula

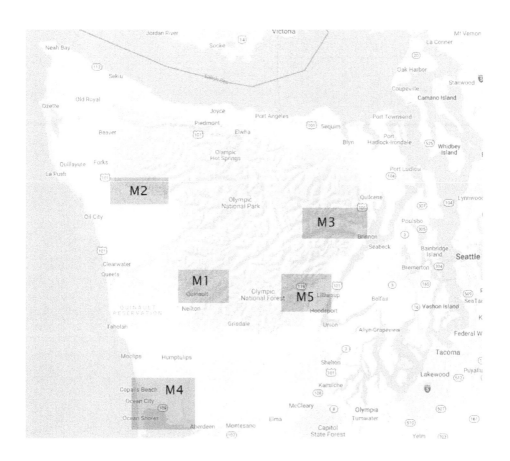

Jason M. Burke

Notes:

Jason M. Burke

Lake Quinault M1

Lake Quinault lies 40 miles to the north of Hoquiam and is about a 47-minute drive. Turn onto South Shore Road just north of Neilton. There are signs abound. This shouldn't be hard. North Shore Road, cleverly, lies just to the North. Remember, if you're merely circling the lake, you'll have to turn from one road onto the other (South Shore to North Shore, North Shore to South Shore) and you cross the North Fork of the Quinault River on a very obvious bridge. There are other roads that continue on into the mountains (unexplored by me).

While this route is enjoyable while approached from either direction, don't skip the old mercantile in Amanda Park. Assuming it is still in operation, the landmark store has antique wooden floors that are creaky and ever-so buckled with age.

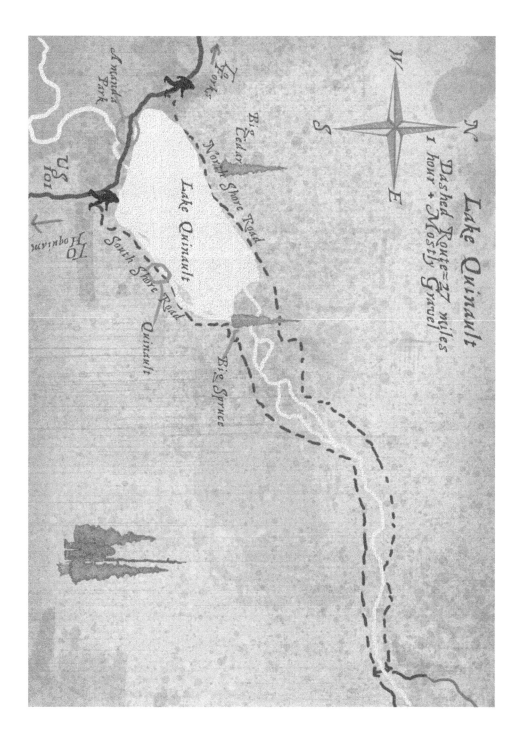

Jason M. Burke

The Hoh Rainforest M2

The turnoff to this road is a hearty 91 miles to the northwest of Hoquiam and will take nearly 2 hours. It's about an hour and a half to the southwest of Port Angeles and 70 miles. It's close to Forks though! From the southerly approach, driving northbound on US 101, watch for the Hoh Oxbow Campground, then the Hoh River's literal, physical Oxbow and then signs for the Hoh Rainforest Visitor Center. Follow the Upper Hoh Road for a leisurely Bigfoot drive. From the north, heading south, the turnoff is 13 miles south of Forks from US 101.

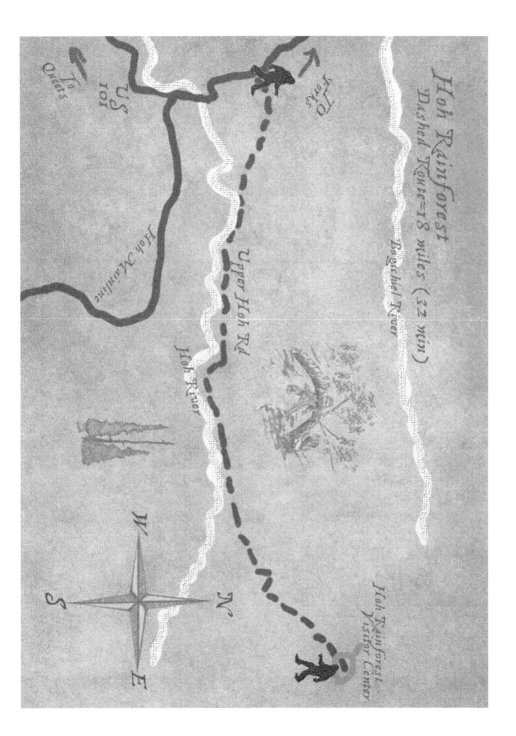

Jason M. Burke

Dosewallips Road M3

Dosewallips Road heads westwardly from US 101 a scant one mile North of Brinnon and 11 miles south from Quilcene if you're approaching from the north.

Jason M. Burke

Dekay Road M4

Approach Dekay Road (and Ocean Beach Road) from either town, Copalis Beach (WA 109) or New London (US 101). Copalis Beach Road turns into OBR at Copalis Crossing (another tiny town). Don't fret the details, wandering onto another road may yield an encounter with the Cowman. You've been warned, though.

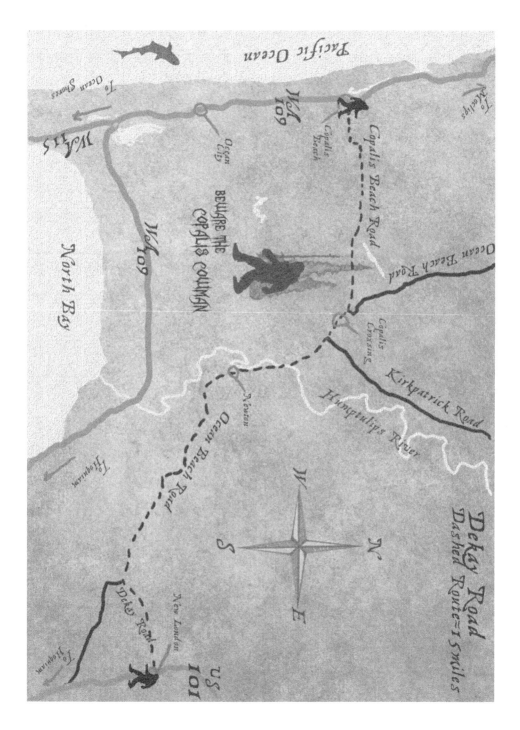

Jason M. Burke

Lake Cushman M5

Turn from US 101 onto WA 119 in Hoodsport. There should be plenty of signs.

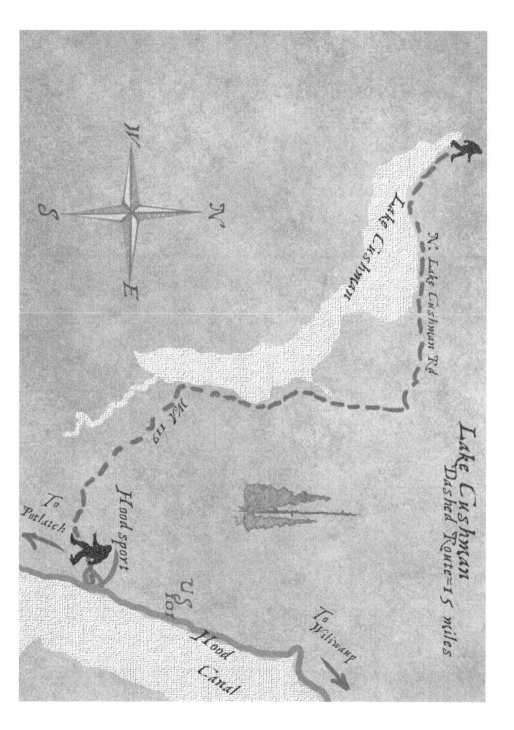

Jason M. Burke

Northern Cascades

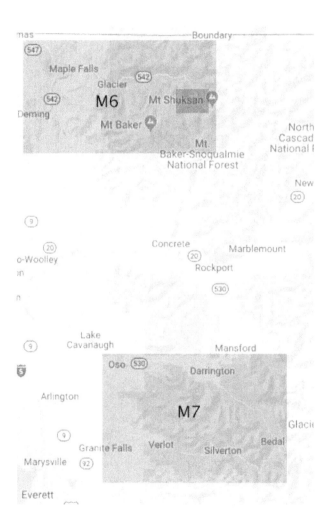

Notes:

Mount Baker M6

The area is easily reached from Bellingham via WA 542. There are signs abound. I've mapped to the ski area on Mount Baker but the road continues from there a short distance with plenty for you to explore. The drive was particularly beautiful in the fall.

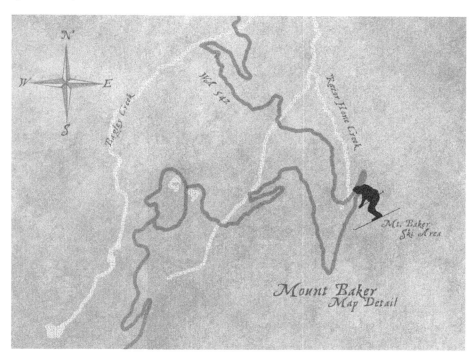

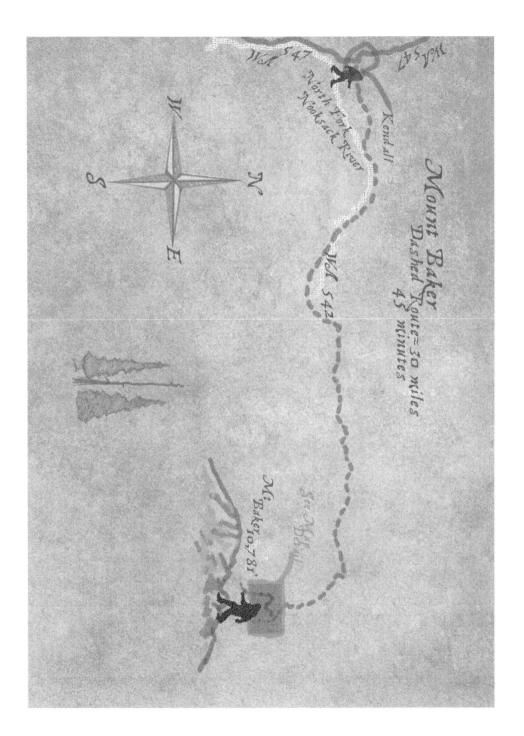

Jason M. Burke

Barlow Pass M7

Plan for a good chunk of the day because there are so many photo ops on this scenic loop. Between Barlow Pass and White Chuck Road, the route is entirely gravel. This is about 14 miles and will take you about 45 minutes driving at a speed which is sane. Any Summer Thursday you'll find campers staking out their best sites on the river. If you want to find yourself alone, explore in the rain, in the off-season, and Tuesday through Wednesday. Some combination of those circumstances or "all of the above" should give you a drive which offers both solitude and mountain beasts. The road is closed after the first snow well into the spring.

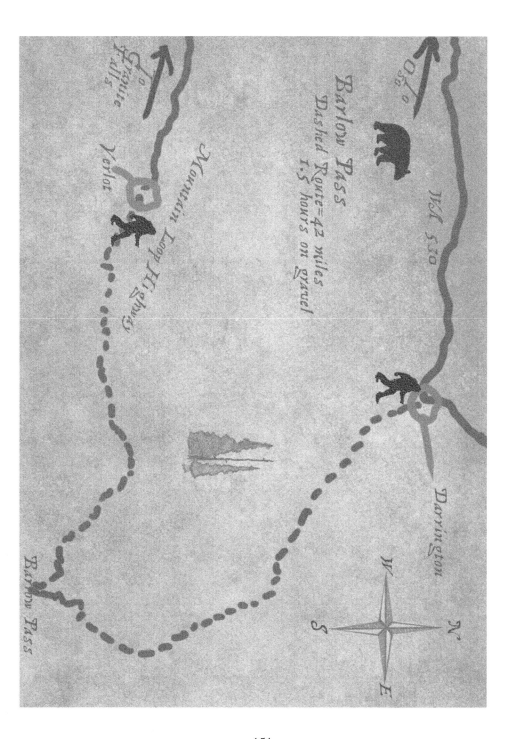

Jason M. Burke

Southwest Washington

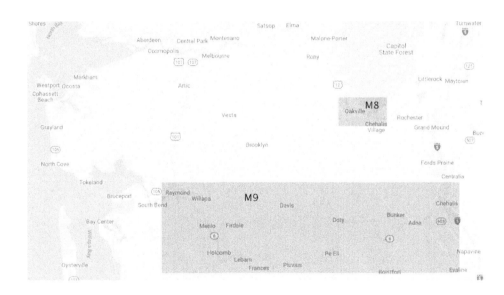

Notes:

Jason M. Burke

Capitol Forest M8

I don't *think* you'll get lost… Being a state forest there are many, many logging roads. There were far too many for me to coherently illustrate on the map. Getting lost, though, should afford you the best opportunity for a chance encounter with Sasquatch. The route I drove took me off of US 12 west of Oakville on Capitol Forest Road. A large blue sign marks the forest entrance. The exploration is up to you. I approached it in search of a through-passage intending on exiting somewhere on the north side. I found myself on Waddell Creek Road. I headed back toward Grand Mound as we were staying at the Great Wolf Lodge. It was purely by accident that I drove through the Mima Mounds Preserve.

You can't miss the mounds. They're as obvious as they are mysterious. As I researched, I was unable to find a single, definitive explanation for how the mounds were created. They are likely, according to the majority of theories, to have been caused naturally by geologic influences. Fringe theories range from extraterrestrials to early man. Pocket gophers, oft celebrated for bringing life back to the nearby Mount Saint Helens blast zone, have even been hypothesized as the builders. Native Americans are known to have built mounds but there isn't any archeological evidence (none that I could find) available to suggest they are responsible for these mounds. Bones, tools, and other human relics are notably absent. This isn't the only occurrence where mysterious mounds and Sasquatch share the same landscape. I don't suggest they're connected by any other force than coincidence but it is an intriguing coincidence, to say the least. I encourage you to judge for yourself.

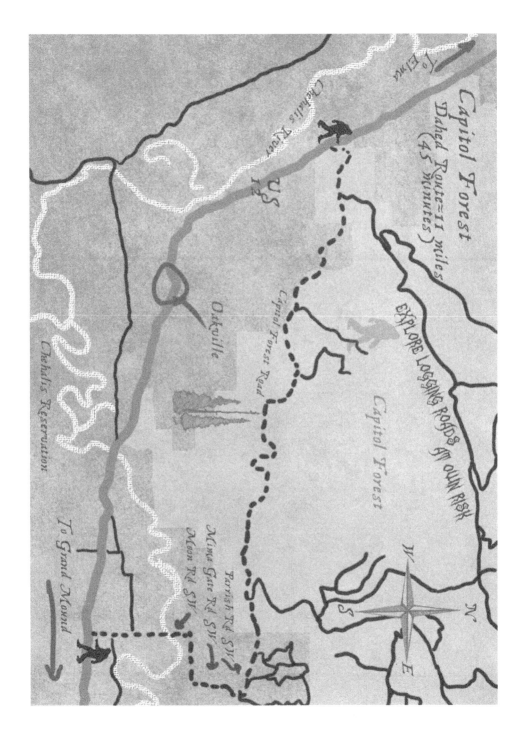

Jason M. Burke

Chehalis to Raymond M9

This is essentially just WA 6 from either the US 101 side or the I-5 side. This area is thoroughly, thoroughly wired for weird.

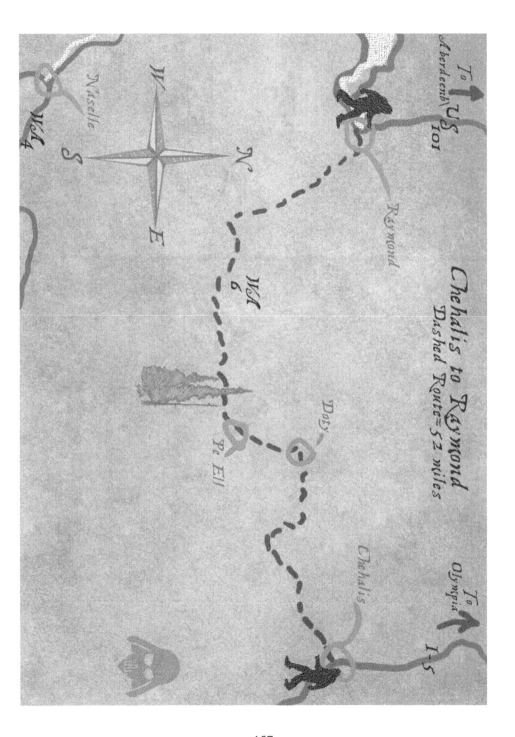

Jason M. Burke

Land of the Skookum

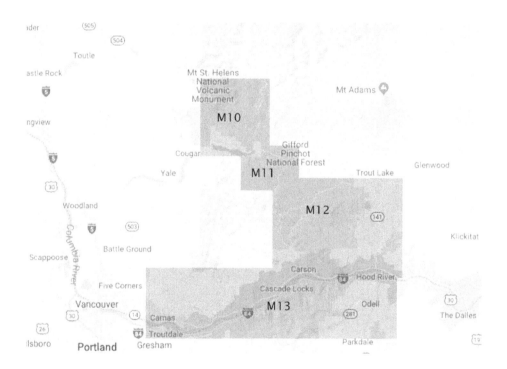

Notes:

Jason M. Burke

Thar be Mountain Devils Here M10

You're looking for the towns of Yale and Cougar. WA 503 will turn into NF-90 (a Forest Service Road) and you'll follow that to NF-83. NF-83 will take you to several ape-related trailheads.

This will be as close to Ape Canyon as many will dare to venture. I believe this area will begin to yield sightings in the future as the habitat recovers from the 1980 blast.

Jason M. Burke

Curly Creek Road M11

This is a fun cutoff road between NF-90 and Meadow Creek Road. You can find the northern approach 23 miles east of Cougar.

Curly! Straight! Curly! Straight!

Secretly Seeking Sasquatch

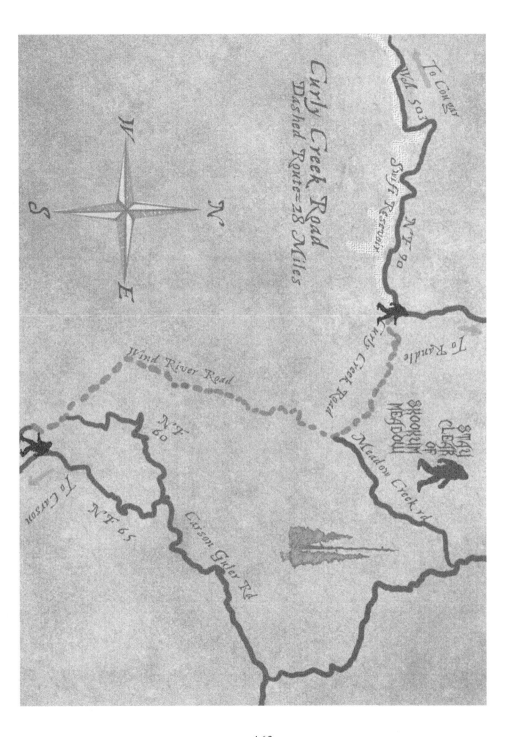

Jason M. Burke

Wind River Road M12

There's a lot of snow here in the winter but the payoff is unapparelled views of Mount Adams and a crack at encountering a legend. Explore headed North out of either Carson (Wind River Rd) or White Salmon (WA 141).

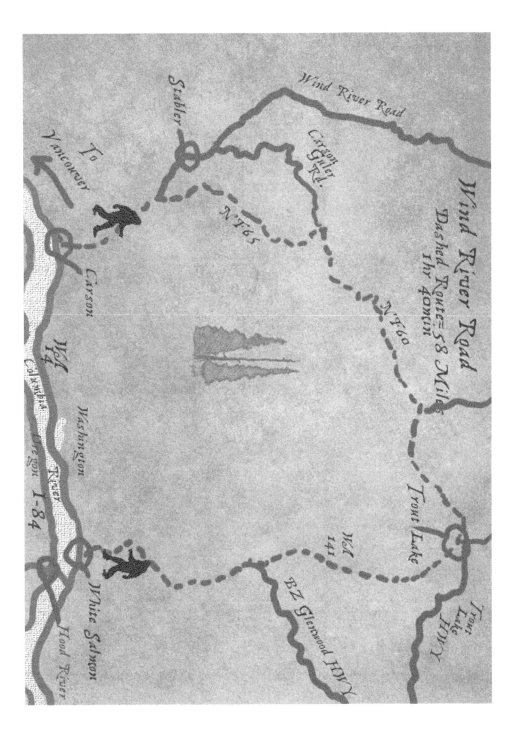

Skamania County M13

This is a paved scenic thoroughfare along the Columbia River, the Washington side. The good one! Just kidding, Oregon. Yours is good too.

In the old Bigfoot episode of *In Search Of*, this is where the motorists claimed to have encountered the creature.

WA 14 very nearly connects Vancouver to the Tri-Cities.

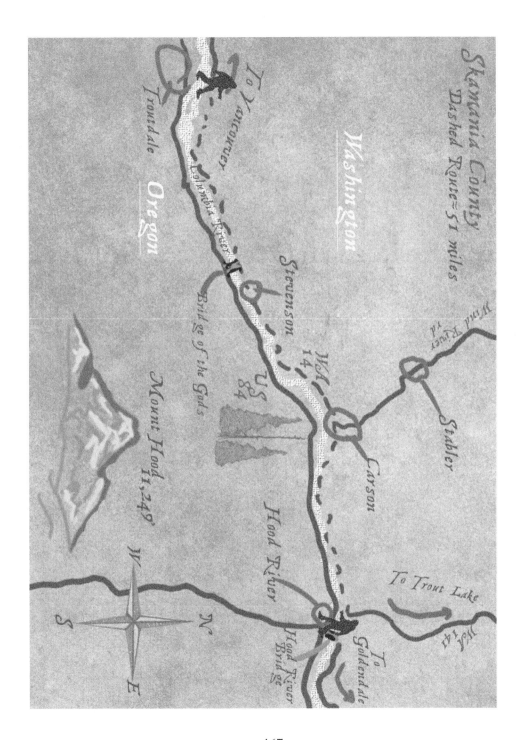

Jason M. Burke

Over the River and Through the Wood (South)

There are many ways to cross Washington's mountains and I urge you cautiously to try them all. The following takes you through the heart of Bigfoot country.

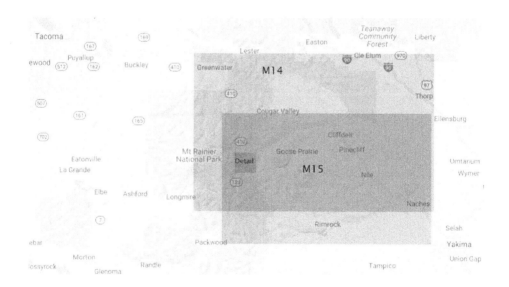

Notes:

Jason M. Burke

Chinook Pass M14

This is most likely Washington's most scenic mountain pass. It will give you outstanding views of Washington's tallest and most photogenic volcano.

Apes inhabit lush volcanic slopes in various parts of the world. It is quite possible that this area offers a similar refuge. Though not as inaccessible as regions in the Amazon, the climate and geography surrounding Mount Rainier aren't any less daunting and most haven't been penetrated by roads. It is the opinion of this author that entire tribes of Sasquatch could inhabit these slopes, forests, mountains, and valleys. They remain hidden because it suits them. Perhaps you'll see one by happenstance.

If you start in Greenwater, it's 19 miles east of Enumclaw on WA 410.

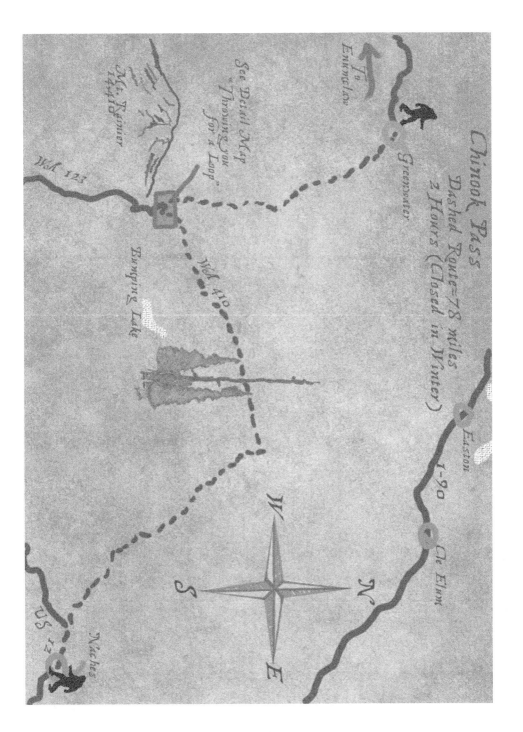

Jason M. Burke

Throwing you for a Loop M15

An alternative approach to seeing the 123 and the highlights of WA 410 would be just to tie the knot. If I were staying in Yakima and had a day to kill, I'd drive this 3-hour-45-minute loop and kill a sunny afternoon.

Naches is 15 miles northwest of Yakima.

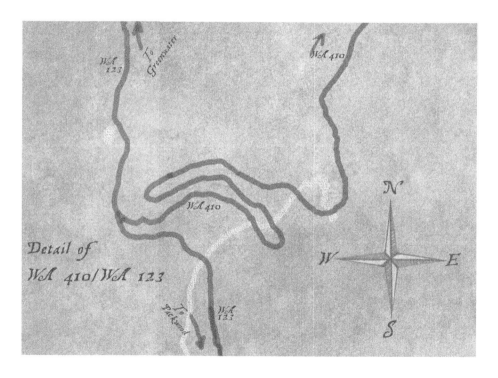

Jason M. Burke

Over the River and Through the Wood (North)

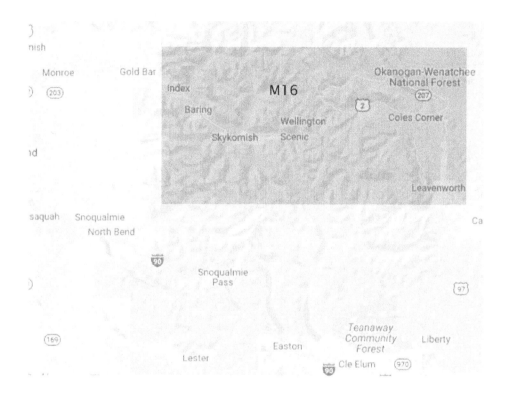

Notes:

Jason M. Burke

Stevens Pass M16

If I took a Bigfoot drive today, it'd be this one. It's a no-brainer approach from either Index or Leavenworth.

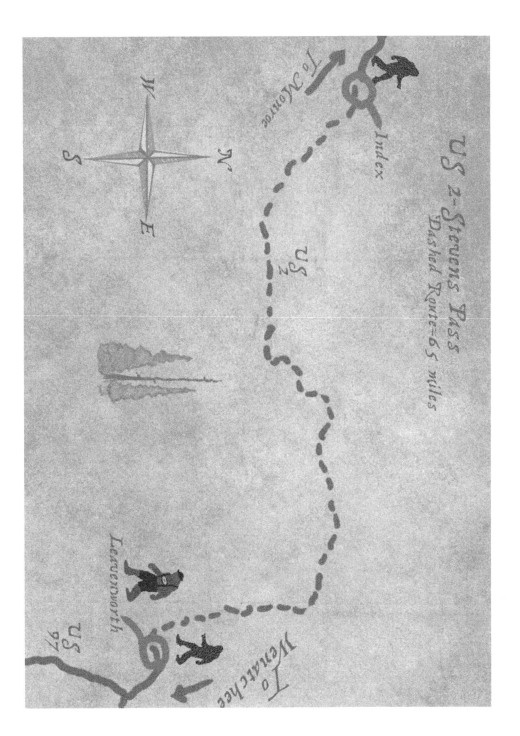

Jason M. Burke

Land of the Okanogan

Notes:

Jason M. Burke

Chopaka Lake M17

One of the weirder places I've been. I found some odd things on the trail. Will you have a similar experience?

From Loomis, follow the Loomis-Oroville Highway a little over 2 miles north. Turn left onto Toats Coulee RD. Go another 1.3 miles and turn right on Chopaka Mountain Rd. This is a dirt road and very steep in places.

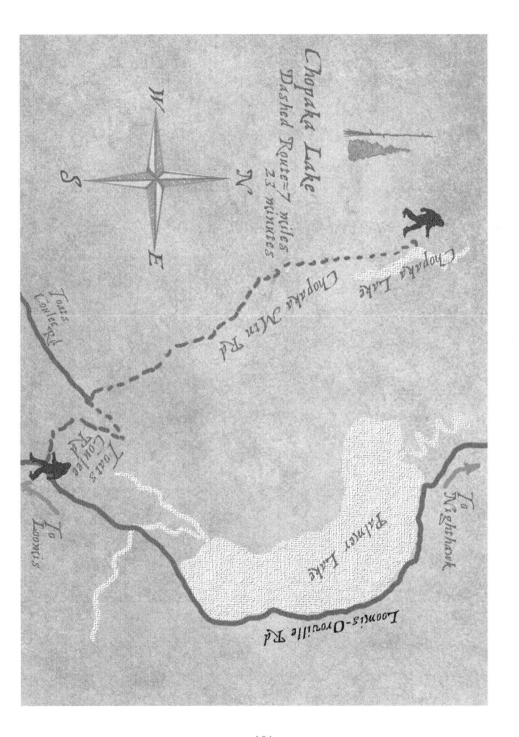

Jason M. Burke

Sherman Pass M18

I've camped and fished here. I haven't seen Sasquatch. Has Bigfoot seen me? The answer is a resounding "probably."

The pass (WA 20) connects Republic and Colville.

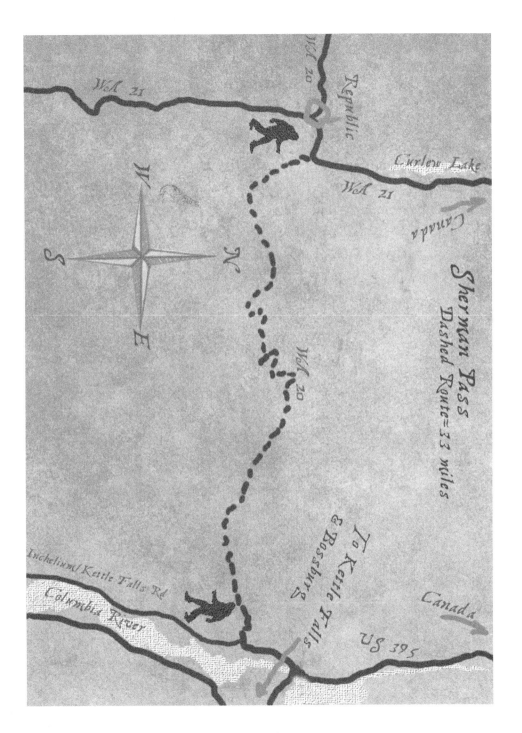

Disautel Pass M19

I'm not going to tell you exactly where to find Smoker's statue. All the same, I hope you find the real thing.

WA 155 heads southeasterly out of Omak.

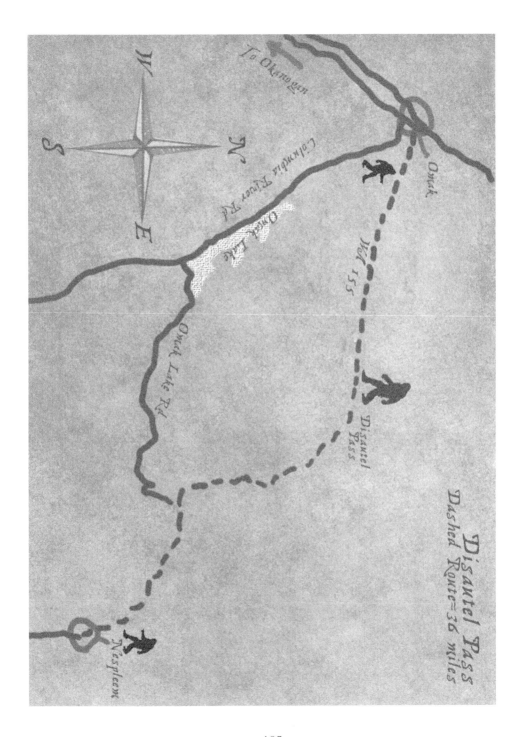

Jason M. Burke

Walla Walla

Notes:

Jason M. Burke

Five Points M20

It's likely you'll explore this area differently than I have recommended and that's perfectly fine. The area is important because some of the best Bigfoot footprints in the world have been collected here and reside in Meldrum's archives.

You follow US 12 northeast out of Walla Walla and pick up Spring Creek Road as you get into the country.

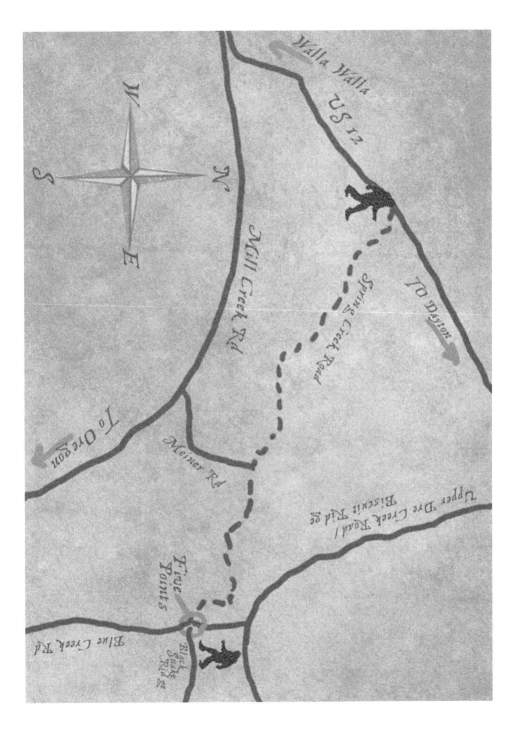

Jason M. Burke

Kendall Skyline Road (KSR) M21

As mentioned in the Walla Walla chapter, this will be the roughest terrain suggested in the book. You'll find this route south of Dayton, WA. Follow the North Touchet Road for about 20 miles. By the time you reach the Bluewood Ski Resort, you'll be in the thick of Bigfoot country.

Bibliography

Arment, C. (2004). *Cryptozoology: Science and Speculation*. Coachwhip Publications.

Baker, S. (n.d.). *The Cowman of Copalis Beach!* Retrieved from Bigfoot Encounters.

BFRO.net. (n.d.). Retrieved from Bigfoot Research Organization: www.bfro.net

Bleiberg, L. (2012, December 14). *usatoday.com*. Retrieved from 10 great places to walk in the shadow of Bigfoot.

Bord, J. a. (2006). *Bigfoot Casebook Updated*. Pine Winds Press.

Borgaard, C. (2010, May 16). *The Daily News: YMCA camp revamped before being Destroyed*. Retrieved from TDN.com: http://tdn.com/news/local/ymca-camp-revamped-before-being-destroyed/article_9f054b62-6161-11df-a1e9-001cc4c03286.html

Coleman, L. (2003). *Bigfoot! The True Story of Apes in America*. New York: Paraview Pocket Books.

Coleman, L. (2004). *Bigfoot!: The True Story of Apes in America*. Paraview Pocket Books.

Coleman, L. (2006, April 21). *Cryptomundo.com*. Retrieved from Bigfoot, Not Bigfeet! Nor bigfoots! Nor sasquatches!

Coleman, L. (2013, December 1). *The Origins of Dr. Wallace Wrightwood, Jacques LaFleur and Harry of Harry and the Hendersons*. Retrieved from Cryptozoonews.

Green, J. (1970). *Year of the Sasquatch*. Agassiz, British Columbia: Cheam Publishing Ltd.

Green, J. (1973). *The Sasquatch File*. Agassiz, BC: Cheam Publishing LTD.

Green, J. (1978). *Sasquatch: The Apes Among Us*. Saanichton, British Columbia: Hancock House.

Green, J. (2004). *The Best of Bigfoot Sasquatch*. Hancock House.

Guttilla, P. (2003). *The Bigfoot Files*. Timeless Voyage Press.

Jeans, C. (Director). (1995). *Secrets of Loch Ness* [Motion Picture].

Jevning, W. (2010). *Notes From the Field, Tracking North America's Sasquatch*. CreateSpace.

Landsburg, A. (Director). (1977). *In Search Of* [Motion Picture].

McGauley, J. (1984, June 13). Is Sasquatch for Real? Well, just maybe according to Evidence. *Grays Harbor Chronicle*. Retrieved from BFRO.net.

Meldrum, J. (2006). *Sasquatch Legend Meets Science*. Tom Doherty Associates.

Napier, J. (1972). *Startling Evidence of Another Form of Life on Earth Now: Bigfoot*. Berkley Medallion Books.

Napier, J. (1973). *Bigfoot: The Yeti and Sasquatch in Myth and Reality*. E.P. Dutton and Co. Inc.

Newsweek. (2016, December/January). What's in a Name. *Newsweek Special Edition: Bigfoot*, p. 15.

Newton, M. (2011). *Strange Monsters of the Pacific Northwest*. Schiffer Publishing, LTD.

Oregon Bigfoot. (n.d.). Retrieved from oregonbigfoot.com: www.oregonbigfoot.com

oregonhistorian. (2016, October 21). *ORHISTORY.com*. Retrieved from The Government is Hiding Bigfoot Bodies!

Place, M. T. (1974). *On the Track of Bigfoot*. Dodd, Mead and Company.

Pyle. (2017). *Where Bigfoot Walks: Crossing the Dark Divide*. Counterpoint.

Roach, J. (2003, April 14). *NationalGeographic.com*. Retrieved from National Geographic News: Elusive African Apes Giant Chimps or New Species?

www.bigfootencounters.com. (n.d.). Retrieved from The Bigfoot Classics.

Made in the USA
Monee, IL
28 September 2021